THE CITY: *A Play by*
PAUL CLAUDEL. *Translated from*
the French by JOHN STRONG NEWBERRY

New Haven: YALE UNIVERSITY PRESS
London: HUMPHREY MILFORD :: OXFORD
UNIVERSITY PRESS ✆ MDCCCCXX

COPYRIGHT, 1920, BY
YALE UNIVERSITY PRESS

DRAMATIS PERSONAE

Lambert de Besme
Avare
Lala
Isidore de Besme
Coeuvre
First Deputy
Second Deputy
Third Deputy
Gérin
Thyrsée
Ivors
Citizens and Soldiers

PLACE

Act One

Evening—The gardens belonging to LAMBERT DE BESME *on a height from which one can view the City.*

LAMBERT DE BESME, *seated,* AVARE, *standing.*

Two men enter by the opposite extremities of the garden path and, meeting each other, depart in opposite directions.

LAMBERT: They separate.   One crosses the other, like the warp and the woof.
AVARE: What does it matter to you?
LAMBERT: Everything matters.
There is, in a given area, no movement
Allotted to chance, nor is the stride of man.
I follow it with as studious an eye as that of a sage in the vortex of a whirlwind, intent on the gyrations of the foetus.

(He pauses, considering the City.
Seeking to unite, they cannot accomplish it.
The more they approach, the more the movement is precipitate.
Such is the movement that is found in cities.
AVARE: Seclusion has made you philosophical.
LAMBERT: Has a new ministry been formed?
AVARE: Lambert, you know that questions weary me.

5

LAMBERT: No one wishes to serve. That is the singular thing. They must in the end decide to call from retirement . . .

(Silence.

. . . Lambert de Besme. They have no other course.

(Enter a man pushing a small baby-carriage, a woman with a child on her arm, and a young boy who walks swinging his arms.

AVARE: And what of these?

LAMBERT: They are out walking, following the path that has the form of a figure eight.

They will return by the same road.

These wretched shadows come to our shades a moment
To augment their opacity.

—Look, the lights of the city begin to shine! Listen!
How many feet are here! All stirs. Each lamp illumines.

The city is resplendent with a fabricated light.

(The glow of the City is seen.

AVARE *(passionately)*: May I live to see the quenching of that light! *(In a lower tone)*: May I live to see the quenching of that light!

LAMBERT: Avare!

AVARE: O weariness, weariness!

LAMBERT: It is the hour when through the streets there pours a throng of white-faced men in sombre garb
And in heaven appears the multitude of the stars.
It is enough that we should be seated
Here. The heavens above our heads

6

And the city of men at our feet serve us for spectacle.

AVARE: O Night!

Would that I might receive the veritable night!

LAMBERT: What troubles you, Avare?

AVARE: O wind upon my face! O breath of the astral void!

—Now I hear.

LAMBERT: What do you hear?

AVARE: I hear a bleating, the voice of the sheep, detest-able to the heart of the proud beast.

For men are assembled here in flocks, like sheep

In the pens of the slaughter-house.

And it has its squares and its streets, its wards and dis-tricts.

But outside one only sees a wall, devoid of windows,

And there are cries, and at certain intervals the drains discharge thick streams of blood.

In the name of Heaven, is it not rank in your nostrils? It stinks of excrement and butchery!

And it vomits forth a whorl of sooty smoke

Like a ditch where one burns up fat and bits of wool.

LAMBERT: Peace!

AVARE: My peace is not yours.

I am not to be classed with the worn and fatigued like you, Lambert.

I am green

Like the round acorn planted between two stones.

And I shall force them apart and I shall plunge my arm into the earth profoundly.

(*Silence.*

7

You do not speak?

LAMBERT: I enjoy the sweetness of the night.

AVARE: For you the summertime has lost its purpose.

LAMBERT: To the young the world is merely the echo of battle and the chorus of the Comedy

But to the ultimate secrets only the older man may be admitted,

Sharing already the absolute of the end he envisages.

This is for me the hour of supreme pause.

Let me enjoy the solemn suspense in which my being waits.

AVARE: They say you are going to marry

The girl you have brought up, Lala.

LAMBERT: Invincible sweetness! Even as the summer with excellence

Constrains every flower to fruit (plumping the apple's sphere with the dilation of the juice within),

As, at each entrance into Gemini, in the breast of the multitude

It engenders a new harvest of feelings and desires,

And as it nourishes in you the movements of that sharp and turbulent humour,

So for me, in the contemplation of the end, and in the disposition of a solemn alternative,

The sweetness it insinuates surpasses peace.

AVARE: And this is Lambert de Besme, that puissant politician, this is that leader of men, that shepherd of mighty cities!

LAMBERT: Two fair eyes illumine all my life! I see two eyes turned toward me, two eyes tender and clear.

Two eyes full of joy and love allure me with a promise
that I attempt in vain to analyse. And as for what
I was, listen.

It is more laborious to guide mankind with persuasion
than with the sword.

To plow the multitude and sow it with words

Is an agriculture full of sweats, abounding in il-
lusions; I am weary of that toil.

I have been given a useless faculty, with the love of
order and law:

The insight into man and that regard which pierces to
the quick, perceiving with a glance

The design of spirits as well as that of ears.

Like its fodder, the society of man lives through the
vegetating belly

And for them the head that thinks is a vain embellish-
ment, and the hand divided into fingers.

Again I say to you; Peace!

AVARE: Peace does not lie in repose. It is not repose
I would have.

My father was a magistrate, a ruddy man with a great,
black beard, a man like the King of Spades,

And he took my mother by force and kept her in rule
and terror.

And I am his son and I march where I must go with the
zeal of a bailiff's underling.

And the blood torments me also.

For suddenly, as I toil at my petty task,

I see peonies in a bowl of brass with their colour in
the water;

9

And I hear the cry of a woman, and all my heart is
    violently compressed, like a wheel that they clamp
    when they have moistened it.
Or I smell the odour of smoking meat!
Or the summer paints itself on my spirit, as if from
    the close-shut room I saw between the shutters em-
    erald boughs.

LAMBERT: The City.
            (*He points to the city outspread below them.
            All the lights are lighted. Silence.*

AVARE: It stirs! It lives! Those tenuous lines of light,
    that intersect through all its length and breadth,
Indicate those canals through which there flows the
    matter of humanity. It speaks!
They grovel together, souls and limbs, mingling their
    breaths and their excrements.
O City! O City!
            (*He raises his fist above his head. In the
            centre of the City flames appear which grad-
            ually develop into a great conflagration.*

LAMBERT: What is that?

AVARE: Ah, ah! Another one!

LAMBERT: Another?

AVARE: Where do you live and what is this you babble
    of ministries?
Haven't you heard of all these conflagrations? The
    flames break out at every point and no one knows
    whose hand has kindled them.
Now it's a factory and now a store,
A theatre, a residence, a school,

Or a ministry with its five stories crammed with papers
    that flame!

It catches all at once from attic to foundations, and the
    roof collapses and vomits flames like an erupting
    crater,

And here and there, at night, one sees the sullen fire
    snoring in cellars.

LAMBERT: It's the Court-House! Look!

AVARE: It is all alight. It burns prodigiously. It bloats
    and swells. It flames like an old tick of straw.

LAMBERT: The fire has mastered everything.

AVARE: Go and be married, blithe and gay! This is the
    moment to marry and to buy a new shirt.

LAMBERT: One would say that you rejoiced.

AVARE: Again! Again! O how this fire flares forth
    and how yellow it appears against the night! You
    won't extinguish it, good people!

    Ho, ho!

LAMBERT: Do you rejoice at such a spectacle?

AVARE: Know that I rejoice,

So much there's not a hair but stands on end and saliva
    jets from my mouth!

LAMBERT: Young man, what man are you?

AVARE: I am the man of astonishment.

One day when I was in the home of friends and one
    that I loved was dead,

While men and women cackled,

All at once I felt I was no longer with them and in
    transport of detestation I gave ear, and I softly
    gritted my teeth,

Thinking that I was imprisoned with these people, and the desire came over me to set alight the four corners of this place of lies:

That I might be alone.

I will do it, for I bear within me a force like the rigour of love!

Look at the city of men! They build themselves houses of stone

And make rooms and stories and flights of stairs, and o'er all they set a roof,

And they make a door below; and the workman supplies it with a lock; and the master clinks the key of it in his pocket.

I knew a wealthy man who thus constructed a house, and at night, when he had retired,

He died in his toilet-room.

They all will die, and death has no name among them.

But I, I will unveil it, and I will establish it in glory,

And I will plant a light before its door which is like the orifice of a city.

And they shall not pass the threshold one by one, but shall flow down like melted snow; suddenly they shall descend, all together like leaves, like flocks of birds!

I will strike this habitation of corruption,

And like the bailiff who appears driving back the people, that the ceremony may be consummated,

I will make recoil from the spot the human race.

The hour has come! And that is why I am seized with joy at the sight of this conflagration,

12

Like a man, who, fixing his eyes on the dark, beholds a
shining light.

(He goes out. Pause.

LALA (*appearing before* LAMBERT): It is I.

(Silence.

Have you nothing to say?

LAMBERT: The same warning

Each time that before my eyes you succeed to your
image;

Even as the prisoner in the depths of earth,

At the muffled rolling of the drum, is ignorant whether
the sound comes from above or below,

Or as, from his seat in the solitary room, the old man
is aware

Of the sigh of the door that opens on the night.

But shall I describe to you, O most beautiful young girl,
that

Which I feel when I behold you?

LALA: Pain or pleasure?

LAMBERT: I cannot tell. A sudden sadness.

But of so voluptuous a sort that at first one does not
know that it has become this secret hilarity;

Something stronger than forgetfulness, frailer than
sleep;

A vivacity quick and new; the bitterness and amaze-
ment

Of those old, dreadful days;

A perfect alleviation; the birth of profound desires,

Yet nothing hard or strained; a tender and humble
sentiment

13

That consoles and penetrates; a mysterious refection.

LALA: Anything else?

LAMBERT: An obscure terror.

LALA: It is probable, O my adopted father, that you are in love with me.

LAMBERT: So be it. There is the label attached.

LALA: What do you wish of me?

LAMBERT: O fairy Lala, daughter of the fern-seed,

You pose a question to which you have ill accustomed me

For, as in the fabulous tale of the Old Man and the White Cat, from the first day that you came, a little violin-player, to waken me from my sombre afternoon repose,

I am the master no more. And you do not trouble much to find out what I want, nor to make clear

That which you want of me.

But your smile illuminated all the house,

From the single crystal mirror to the kitchen's copper pans, to the glasses of the dining-room.

And I, hard man accustomed to the sinister virile face, when the strong hand grips it by the beard,

I marvelled at this little child that had been given me,

And my eyes on your pure face, when those faithless lips unclosed,

I needs must obey, knowing only what you summoned me to do.

O Lala, if it is pleasing in your sight, let us determine this point, and let us assure each other that in our home we shall live together always,

And, according to the custom of others, let us agree to
be husband and wife.

LALA: It is true, O adopted father, that I should never
know how to love any man that was not you.

For who offered me a home? And since that one time
when it was given to you to be embraced, between
my bow and violin, by me,

(And it is the violin that makes me bow my head when
I wish to laugh and not any faithlessness),

Who has brought me up and nourished me? It is only
right that I should love you.

LAMBERT: Come with me! By a marriage mysterious,
like that of the violoncello and the organ, by a harmony of subtle counterpoint,

Of old I thought there might be happiness between a
man and a woman.

Incontinent let us dwell in the great and ancient house

That I have in mind, on the flank of the valley between the elm and the larch.

Always caressed by the sweetest sun its walls retain
the dryness and solidity of rock.

Within would the mystery be, something ripe and profound.

And through the corridors, filled with tempered light,
and through the peaceful rooms,

You would inhale a latent redolence, a hint of wax and
roses.

On the right, between the chestnuts, would be the farm

With its animals and tools; and the stables and the

dairy, and the mangers filled with straw and hay,
the barns and the granaries.

On the left there is an enormous garden with every sort
of plant and curious tree

Whose properties we should explain to one another,
And about us, all creation.

Do not scorn me because my youth is over.

For in youth man is only hardness, egoism, brutality,
lust, the bitter brew of newly vintaged wine.

Goodness alone is a treasure, and if you love me, O
Lala, to you I will open my heart which is like the
heart of a father,

And I will give you the honey with its comb, O my
daughter!

Thus shall our marriage august be like the nuptials of
Jupiter and the Nymph.

LALA: No. I wish you to remain here, erect in the
battle.

LAMBERT: Do you then consent to have a wish for me?

LALA: They say that these men will come to you tonight.

LAMBERT: Well?

LALA: It is my wish that you cause to appear before
them

The woman their master has chosen.

(*Pause.*

LAMBERT: Be my consolation.

I saw you last autumn, child, and there was earth on
your cheeks. I saw your face between the ripened
apples, green and red.

Come, that I may lie with you, and that I may hold you
the whole night long.

LALA: Do you really wish to marry me?

LAMBERT: I am almost old, and I know that you cannot
love me.

Would that I were a man of the people, for they live
simply side by side in friendship.

The ewe gives wool and milk, and the earth produces
poppies with the grain.

But the male is fruitful also, and to whom will he give
food, like a nutriment that one shares amid the darkness, until one's teeth are grown?

As for me, sterile I live; do not allow me to die.

I have no wife and I shall have no children!

Living the dust has been my lot, and couched, the earth.

LALA: I must confess to you, friend, I love you well.

Marry me, and I shall be your wife, for there is no
one but you that I can love.

And you will not be sad, for I am with you forever.

LAMBERT: O Lala, is this truth?

LALA: All the same let us go to throw buns to the carp
in the basin of the Pleiades.

(They go out.

(Enter from opposite sides ISIDORE DE BESME
and COEUVRE.

BESME: Who is there?

COEUVRE: Isidore de Besme, I salute you.

BESME: Welcome, Coeuvre, into my walled garden.

COEUVRE: From the moment I enter it I possess

This garden, Besme, more than you yourself.

With its trees and its rocks and its terraces,
And its perfumes of blossoms superposed on the odour
of its leaves,
It occupies a certain place in the shade, like a poem
submerged in the thought.
Like a bouquet disposed in a vase profound,
This garden, steeped in the night, affords a refuge.
Into its depths I plunge.
After the frightful agitation
Of the City, in the implacable light, how grateful is
this dark to my wounded eyes! O shades, how your
access is full of consolation!

BESME: Have you also a grief to hide?

COEUVRE: It's true; yes, Besme, I think what you say is
true. I suffer.

BESME: Are you not certain of it?

COEUVRE: A musician is more concerned with finding
the harmonies of the note he hears
Than with measuring its vibrations.

BESME: I confess it, Coeuvre, you fill me with amaze-
ment!
As for me, who am wise in material things,
From every substance I seize between my hands I am
ready to disengage the elements and to define the
properties and functions.
And, as with a number used in the operation of an
eternal arithmetic,
I have assured myself that no portion of this sum is
unproductive or vain.

And likewise each living being has his predestined task
    with its provision of energy.
This is a certain and satisfying thing.
But you, Coeuvre, what are you, and what purpose do
    you serve?
You have not the apology of the charlatan, who mounts
    his chair to amuse the public,
For the fool takes no joy in your words, the sage finds
    no instruction there.
Their meaning eludes the one, and the other fails to
    grasp
Their connection, like a stalk lost in profound glooms.
COEUVRE: O Besme, to know what I am and what I say,
You need another science,
And for its acquisition, forgetting an impious logic,
    it suffices to open your eyes to that which is.
O Besme, if this leaf grows sere
It is not because the obstructed channels wither,
Nor that, falling, it may house and feed the seeds and
    larvae round the foot of the tree.
It turns yellow to appropriately afford to the neighbor-
    ing leaf, which is red, the complement of the neces-
    sary note.
All things are present, and between the future and the
    past there is only progress on a single plane.
And when you demand the purpose that I serve, you
    commit a fault, you confound the categories.
Of what service is the colour of your hair?
Of what service is the orchid in the heart of the virgin

wood, the sapphire that no miner's sledge will ever free from its ore?

Unknown of men, the Being who has made us, and maintains us in the light of his countenance,

Knows us, and secretly we contribute to his glory.

BESME: O you that like the tongue reside in a place obscure!

If it is true, like the welling stream that gushes from the earth,

That Nature has unstopped a spring of words between the lips of the poet,

Make clear to me whence comes this breath by your mouth transformed into words.

For when you speak, like a tree that with all its leaves

Stirs in the silence of Noon, within our hearts peace imperceptibly succeeds to thought.

By means of this song without music and this word that has no voice, we are put in accord with the melody of the world.

Naught you explain, O poet, but all things grow comprehensible through you.

COEUVRE: O Besme, I do not speak according to my will, but I conceive in sleep.

And whence I obtain this breath I could not tell you. It is the breath that is supplied to me.

Dilating this void within me, I open wide my mouth,

And, having inhaled the air in this legacy of himself through which man exhales each moment the image of his death,

I give back in its stead an intelligible word

And having said it, I know what I have said.
BESME: Thus, bit by bit, I contrive to make your trouble
    manifest.
    Is it not true, O Coeuvre, that every word is either a
    response or calls for one?
    And that is why all verse, your own excepted,
    Has rhythm or rhyme, admits or comprehends
    An element exterior to itself.
COEUVRE: It is true.
BESME: But you,
    Whom do you interrogate, or to whom do you make
    reply?
    Where is that exchange, that mystic respiration, of
    which you spoke just now.
COEUVRE: It is true, O Besme.   You have rightly
    guessed my grief.
    I am beset with doubt, and in terror I hear the echo.
    Each word is an interpretation of love, but though love
    may fill my heart,
    Who loves me, or who can say that I have loved him?
    Such is the wine of the vine that some drink sweet,
    Others lay down in their cellars in reserve,
    Still others distill to form an ardent brandy, through
    the transformation of the sugar.
BESME: Thus from all men you hold yourself aloof,
    lacking the human bond
    Of mutual interest or exchange of words.   O Coeuvre,
    would it not be better to place this wine on the table?
    Bring to the common feast your part.
    Be not among us useless and excommunicated!

21

COEUVRE: Excommunicated from what faith?

(*Pause.*

BESME: There are no more gods and their words are as the wind.

No priest, with altar at belly, honours the starry Night and the double doors of the Sun.

In place of the idol who, o'er the scent of wine and the smoke of the holocaust,

Expanded nostrils of wood and eyes of porcelain,

Man himself has mounted the pedestal.

And the world in the immensity of its herbage has been delivered to him, and he has girdled it with roads of steel.

And, at the banquet, each one takes his seat fronting the altar sacred to himself.

And as for me, myself, Besme, who would you say I am?

COEUVRE: The countenance, the beard, the fire of the eye betray

Saturn, the patron of inventors and gardens set with trees.

Certainly no one can ever reproach you with ranking among the good-for-naughts,

Profound mime, new Prometheus,

You that probing and imitating Nature's most secret movements,

Have made them serve the purposes of man.

Some day I have no doubt you will harness the planets like mules,

Adjust your turbines to the ocean's tide,

And utilise the force of mounting sap and the reper-
cussion of light
To grind our grain and weave our shirts.

BESME: It is true, Coeuvre, beyond all chance of doubt.
And that is one reason I may well be called the Father
of the City.
For even as the aquatic birds assemble in the marshes,
Or the factories congregate by the torrent's bed,
It is thus the crowds of workers have seated themselves
beside the rivers of force that I caused to gush from
the earth.
You have seen in the centre of my gardens my reser-
voirs like seas:
I have reared the embankment, I have built the cisterns.
For it is I
Who give water to the city, and motive power, and
light.
And I stand here like the fly-wheel, turning upon itself,
to which the belt is attached,
Through all the city animating the people of the forges,
the saws, the hammers, the mills, rank upon rank and
story upon story, the world of lathes and looms.
You said just now, O Coeuvre, that I should find a way
to yoke the strength of the spring and the mounting
sap;
But that of thought is stronger.   And it is in my
thought that all the city
Finds the principle of its activity and life.
Gaze through the darkness, Coeuvre, the place of man
Sends back a glow like the female sea.

Through me, through me, the city of men unfolds itself about me

That I may find pleasure there and that they may receive my help.

COEUVRE: Yes, Besme.

BESME: It is thus that I have been made a god.

Do you understand? Not a right hand here is aided
by a left hand

Which does not work for me, not one of these millions
of heads that grovel at my feet

Which does not pay me tribute, no slightest atom of
matter

Whence the operation of man cannot engender gold

For me.

For even as the Sun with its rays envelops all the world,

It is so that the subtle and splendid gold is needful to
produce

That universal enjoyment, like a consideration of the
spirit,

For which I am constituted among men.

COEUVRE: You are great, Besme!

BESME (*violently*): Would to heaven that I had not
been born!

Or that I had not received this fatal gift of vision

Through which, in the midst of darkness void of
measure and dimensions, I hold my own light!

COEUVRE: What do you mean?

BESME: You are not unaware of those sly and patient
lures

Through which a dreary voluptuousness, that slowly penetrates our secret sense,

If the burdened spirit allows itself once to yield, in a moment entangles and captivates the imagination and the will.

As for me, I know a blacker evil, a slavery more sad.

COEUVRE: What?

BESME: The evil of death, the knowledge of death.

It was while I was working, peacefully inscribing a row of figures on the page,

That this thought for the first time filled me, like a sombre lightning.

Now I do this, and in a little while I shall do something else.

In a little while I shall be gay, or I shall be sad, good, wicked, greedy, prodigal, patient, captious,

And I am living till I am no more.

But as each of these adjectives reposes upon that permanent verb, in what does my identity continue?

A torpor invades me, dissolution divides my fingers from the pen.

The desire for work, the motive for work, have left me and I remain inert and motionless.

I exist. I think.

O that I could not think!

Necessity constrains and amalgamates mankind.

But I being rich am free, being free I am alone, and, alone, I support upon myself alone the burden of all death, the total malediction of all mankind and of every living being.

COEUVRE: You speak of the hidden evil. What is the good of living?

—I distinguish the scent of lilies.

BESME: A peach is no more than a turnip between the teeth; the hair of woman seems to me like the bristles of an ass.

I drink the water of the chilly marsh, I quench my thirst at the cup of death.

Know that at times I descend from here at night and enter the city, and, through deserted streets, in the midst of a sleeping people, I wander like a lost soul.

O stones!

O habitation funereal and derisive! O human place where man has arranged to be alone with himself! O tomb, how inextricable are thy ways!

Man will not come forth from the sepulchre he has constructed for himself.

(Pause. The moon rises.

COEUVRE: Yet the poplars tremble above us. The moon rises.

Opening my eyelids and closing them again, I see, turn by turn, with my eyes and in my thought, illuminated space.

O the splendour of the full sea,

When the shadow of great clouds is portrayed on the shining solitudes.

I salute thee, O Queen of the Night!

(Pause.

BESME: Hail, Bearer of Light!

COEUVRE: Ovation to the resplendent moon, eye of
glory!

You manifest, without destroying it, the mystery of the
sky with its extent.

For, like the new possessor of a palace who visits it,
torch in hand,

Luminous you march across the hall of the empty
Night.

And although you cherish other abodes, all water

Descending, wild,

Or domestic beneath the leaves, the flour-mill and the
saw-mill reared below the moving wheel;

And you favor new lovers who, in mutual embrace,

Have lost all power of parting from each other,

And the grassy stream, cycnean;

—Love

This garden midst the plain that shows only aridity,
Diana!

I salute thee with, not offering aught beside,

       (*He takes a handful of earth and pours it out.*

This libation of earth.

The new blooms render you incense, Lamp of Sleep.

                 (*Enter* LALA.

LALA (*to* COEUVRE): What has happened to you, my
master, since the days when you taught me Latin?

For, lids half-lowered, you listened, while, one arm
above the book, I expounded

The sports of Lavinia or the metamorphoses of the
sisters of Phaeton.

But now it is you who expound

This book that you have within you, and the world,
Your school, has become your scholar.
And it is not the thrush or the nightingale that sings!
But like a river that flows from the mouth of the
earth,
Intelligible words, like water, gush forth from the pro-
foundness of your thought.
And through them we ascend, as to a spring, towards
you.
COEUVRE: Young girl, I am well aware that you can
laugh and mock.
Truly I know that I am, through all the streets of this
city, an object of astonishment and derision.
For what is my place among men, of what whole am I
the part, and, outside of myself,
For what purpose is it essential, that which essentially
I am?
You accused me, Besme, just now and your reasons
have convinced me.
LALA: Is this true, O Coeuvre?
COEUVRE: It is not what once I thought.
When I was quite young, when, in an instant I felt
the flower unfold, and my thought was like a garden
into which one enters
To see what has sprouted since the night before, in
my innocence I thought
All this was mine and that I could do as does the
peasant woman
Who goes to see and choose what she can bear to
market Saturday,

The fowls and the eggs, and the butter, and the fruit, and the vegetables, and the flowers.

What divine conversation, I thought, I am going to have with men!

LALA: Well?

COEUVRE: For then I judged, young girl,

That there was nothing of ourselves that was not susceptible of communication.

And if the word is a food, it is thus that different nutriments have been bestowed.

And there are some of these that man prepares

Himself, like bread, from raw grain and other things requiring to be cooked;

There are some that he grinds and mashes, some where the tongue alone performs the task;

And others like milk, and others

That melt in the mouth of themselves, like butter and sugar.

And, driven by the sound within, I wished to propound to the world a soluble phrase, a phrase delectable,

In order to nourish, like a profound stomach, the memory and the intelligence, like a mouth that is edged with lips and teeth.

Thus it is that once, calling forth a vision from my heart, walking or seated, to my eager ears I related my identity,

Invoking the heavens and the earth, and this world into which I had been admitted, up to that which stretched itself over Nature,

Night, like the shade of a tree.

And the volume I conned was not between the hands
of any master, and all arrayed in joy I took no heed
of women.

But now like the oak of Zeus that is filled by the
prophetic wind and cannot quit the soil it embraces
with multifarious roots,

I do not stir from the spot and none attends my voice.

And it is in vain that I wait. In my waiting I grow old,
and silence

Is not comparable to the stark oblivion in which I find
myself.

And that is why, useless in life, I do not feel my foliage
foreign to death.

LALA: O stupid man, why speak of death when you live?
And, tell me, do you know that you will die?

As for me, I am joyous and 'tis enough. I ask no more
of life.

For the sun is given to men for the day and the moon
is given for the night.

And behold, it is full, it shines in the midst of the sky,
like a rose!

I salute you, O Moon! Barefoot, in the silence of
midnight, I shall dance before you, like a white pea-
cock!

For in the spring you illuminate the flowers and in the
autumn the pears that hang in hundreds along the
walls.

—And all this garden is yours, Monsieur de Besme?

BESME: It is mine. It is the plot of grass into which,
like a glow-worm, I have withdrawn myself.

LALA: You must give me this garden. Do you know I
am going to marry your brother? We have only
just agreed to be engaged.

BESME: Has he at last been guilty of this folly?

LALA: This folly?

BESME: It is the kitten that plays with a golden sun-
beam!

May I never suffer the misfortune of being controlled
by that child, a woman,

Who varies like the movement of the eyes!

For Lambert has no thought outside of this desire,

And if I say to him, "Dolt, at your age, what have you
to do with a wife?"

He makes no answer, but, bowing his head with a secre-
tive air, he smiles ironically.

LALA: But is it not right that I should be glad, since
there is someone who loves me?

Yes, and that, being a woman,

From the very fact of my presence, wherever my feet
bear me,

I bring joy, I carry love!

And behold my youth is not in vain, and I have granted
to someone the right to take me by the hand.

But while I am still alone and free I shall wander like
a bird that sings in sudden phrases!

What words with an inviolate lip

Shall I exchange with this night that I respire, and by
the accents of what voice

Shall I replace the dream of sleep?

I watch when all are sleeping. And though, with no
use of their sense,
They sleep, outside the house
The sun of Night illuminates the earth!
Tell me, Coeuvre, what should I say, for I love and
I am loved. What shall I praise but sleep
Which with a shadowy blow vanquishes our resistance.

COEUVRE: Benediction!

LALA: Benediction
From this sand on which I hold myself erect, to the
sky, to the world of stars
Which reveals itself like a city whose lights we see
from the ocean, to the transcendent waters
Jetting forth from the soil, and to the vast breadth of
the sea!
Benediction to these glooms that silver light
Dissimulates like a bride beneath her veil! Praise!

COEUVRE: Praise!

LALA: To this night of all the nights!

COEUVRE: I will raise my hands in the splendour of the
night!

LALA: I will raise my hands in the splendour of the
night!

COEUVRE: Hail, Sign! Hail, Face! I will praise thee,
O Moon. . . .

LALA: Since thou shinest there, O radiant one!
O thou that testifiest through the night of the sun that
thou beholdest!

COEUVRE: Since, O Face among the eternal habitations,
like a woman,

That one does not see by day, thou dost appear at
the hour of sleep, resplendent,

Or eclipsed, till at evening we may in heaven once more
behold thy sign.

LALA: Hail, Lamp.

COEUVRE: Be blessèd, thou that at thy setting forth an-
nouncest

That the day is ended and that once more the time
has come for sleep.

Thou unbindest the slaves; thou deliverest the adul-
terer from his shame;

And the poor man from his oppression, and the miser
like a child unclasps his hands.

Every eye is closed, every mouth is silent; there are no
more men, nor women, nor masters, nor sages; but
quietly one stretches on one's stomach.

Man sleeps.   The fish sleeps suspended in the liquid
profundity.   He sleeps.

But there are three sleeps that I envy; the last sleep

Of the sick man who has ended his sufferings, and the
slumber of the innocent man unjustly condemned to
death, and the repose

Of the wife who bears in the womb her fruit.

LALA: Blessèd be the splendour of the day, blessèd be
the shadow of the night!

O moon, penetration and aureole, of that which sleeps
and of that which does not sleep; the poacher lying
in wait,

And the son who watches his dying mother and, oppo-

33

site on the wall, sees the shadow of the window and
of the branches;

And the young man with the young girl who, during
the ball at the château, have withdrawn to the em-
brasure of a window (from on high they perceive
the village flattened out in the bottom of the valley),

And the traveller who, returning home at midnight,
sees the white wall of his house, and his vine and
rosebush;

And the betrothed, O Coeuvre, who, having given her
faith, does not know how to take it again.

But you, why is it you do not marry?

COEUVRE: What is the good conferred by marriage,
Lala?

LALA: You will see and you will possess

Your wife in the fold of your arm, and in the extension
of your hands

Your children and the children of your children, boys
and girls.

COEUVRE: Ought I to marry, Besme?

BESME: I do not know. It matters very little.

COEUVRE: Is there any other advantage?

LALA: You will no longer be alone, for a devoted
woman will be with you constantly,

Someone always yours and who will never leave you,
your wife.

COEUVRE: What woman could love me, I being what I
am?

LALA: Many women could love you, Coeuvre.
   But you, have you not a heart that loves?
COEUVRE: All speak to the same effect, and I answer
   never a word.
LALA: But this is true, Coeuvre.
   Why not do as others do, as Nature prompts?
   For it is not good for man to be alone.
COEUVRE: What do you know of Nature? For myself
   This is not the counsel that Nature has given me, the
      spring in its glory and when in the conquering sun
      together there burst into bloom
   The grass, the flowers and the leaf!
   That I should seek a young girl, and not a woman,
   And marry her, and appease my longing thus.
   For such is the thing known as love; the living body of
      the man and woman through this shall find content.
   But the love that I have conceived
   Reposes not in repose and has no knowledge of it.
   This is not the counsel that has been given me!
   But like an animal in the midst of the earth, like a
      horse unbridled that towards the sun launches a hu-
      man cry,
   When, for the first time opening my eyes, I saw the
      world in the freshness of its leaves
   Appear in a sublime proportion, with the order of its
      laws and the complexity of its motion, and in the
      depth of its foundation,
   Like a man who adores, like a woman who wonders,
      I stretched out my hands, and like

35

A Mirror of purest gold restoring unimpaired the total
  image of impinging fire,

I burned with a longing equal to my vision, and, draw-
  ing towards the principle and cause, I wished to see
  and have!

And as for that other frenzied love, if anyone sees himself rejected, or betrayed,

He goes to hide himself, and evermore intent upon this
  one disaster,

He does not know what he says, and is silent unseason-
  ably.

And it is so with me. Alone, like a man made desolate,
  I wander along the roads

Picking up stones and bits of wood, walking submerged
  in thought. Penetrating the forest I shall not go out
  till the evening.

And if anyone is my friend, I am only a friend ambig-
  uously.

But as for the married man, he does not read, and if
  he has time he will talk about his neighbours: and,
  sharing the household bread, he eats his part and
  chews it with satisfaction.

LALA: Do not despise us, O Coeuvre!

COEUVRE: There is no one I despise.

But I am like a man who has recrossed a river, and
  vomiting water arrives at the other side.

And no one understands the tale he tells, and he himself even as he speaks forgets.

But all the region was empty, no man, no beast, no
  sound.

36

And perhaps it is well that the people who hear him do
not understand: for, listening, they perhaps would
cease to work,

And to build themselves houses and fashion doors
therein with zealous industry.

But I, I will undertake my task alone!

I will shake myself like an elephant who, in the morning sets forth to seek a ford.

It is thus that I shall advance, and where I die they
will not find my body.

LALA: As for me, the thing that I dread is solitude.
God grant that I may never be alone!

(*Enter* LAMBERT.

LAMBERT: Have I found you again, Lala?

LALA: Lambert! Defend me from them, for they
mock at me and at you as well.

They say it is folly for you to marry me.

LAMBERT: But do you really consent to marry me?

LALA: Have I not given my answer?

LAMBERT: Answer no more than yes . . .

LALA: I shall answer you presently, Lambert.

LAMBERT: . . . or no. I am not young and I will not re-
ward myself with words alone.

They, they are coming to seek me, presently.

They have driven me out, and now would call me
back and pursue me even to my retreat. All have
abandoned me, but if I return again they shall know
Lambert de Besme!

For I know what should be done and shall not accept
advice.

But if I remodel this house, I wish to have a room there
  for myself.
And in it I shall put my wife, and I shall not let myself
  be dispossessed, and that wife, Lala,
Shall be you, if you answer yes,
Because I love you.
And otherwise I shall not enter that wrecked and falling house and I shall not re-establish the central
  beam. Let it crumble to dust!
Let the four walls bulge and gape and plunge to earth
  and the floors be heaped up one upon another!

(*Long silence.*

BESME: Nothing is.
LALA: Eh? What does he say?
BESME: Nothing is.
LAMBERT: Nothing is?
LALA: What does he mean? Nothing is?
BESME: Nothing is.
LAMBERT: Brother, what lugubrious word has fallen
  from your lips?
You are the eldest of our family and you were the
  wisest and strongest.
And in what you had discovered through your wisdom
  you did not hesitate to put your trust.
For through contact with the effects you have fathomed
  the secret causes.
The ancient gods subdued the animals to the domina-
  tion of man.
But you, like a crafty miller who diverts the course of
  a stream to run his mill,

Have made captive the elemental forces, to the very
   pulsation of life you have adapted the movement
   of your machine.

And you know each thing in its act and operation
   through which, being needful, it is.

But regard this city, for it is you that made it and it is
   for you, rich man, that it was made,

That you might be freed from the burden of toil and
   that like a man in the house he has constructed to
   there enjoy his goods

You might enter into possession of yourself.

And now is this your word? Why, like one that is
   dead, do you withdraw from the life of men?

BESME: Nothing is.

LAMBERT: He repeats the same phrase.

LALA: What? "Nothing," did you say?

This leaf that I grasp, this earth, are these not actual
   things?

And I, do I exist or do I not, and what of yourself,
   Besme?

BESME: Nothing is.

LALA (*kneeling before him and throwing her arms
   around him*): I implore you not to believe it.

BESME (*repulsing her*): Back!

No, woman!

Go, raise the lips of the dead and kiss them on the
   teeth!—Listen, I will repeat the phrase that I ut-
   tered, "Nothing is!"

I have seen and I have touched

39

The horror of uselessness, to that which is not adjust-
ing the proof of my hands.

Nothingness does not lack the power to proclaim itself
through a mouth that can say, "I am."

(This is my spoil and such is my sole discovery.)

COEUVRE: I also speak to you like that young girl. I
implore you not to believe it.

I say this word to you, I who am low and humble
among all men.

BESME: Do you think to constrain me?

COEUVRE: Yes, why can't I do it and why am I not
the Earth

To initiate to my Orgy. Regard the sky when it opens,
when the golden rain descends in the gleam of lightning!

And the winter when one cannot go outdoors.

With closed eyes stand erect in the country at noon,

Or think of the forest in June, O peace profound!
Hear the song of the cuckoo.

Wait, you shall see with your eyes if Spring has come,

When this roaring son of the snow fills all of France
with light

Making stream beneath one's feet the shining waters
thanks to whose agency

The vine grows warm, the grass abounds, and the
flowers and the nourishing pumpkins.

And the rose, steeped in moisture,

Breathing perfume, turns to the torrid star, and you,
turn your heart towards Joy!

Turn, Besme, turn your face towards Joy.

40

BESME: Come, put a balance between us, adjust the
 scales,
And in one pan put the Universe and I will put in the
 other
My doubt, and this it is that will descend.
No, Coeuvre, though Persuasion should stand before
 me, though an effort should fill its throat, more pure
Than the ripple of the spring
Or the voice of the rut when the toad beneath the rick
 speaks with a word of crystal . . .

> *(Enter the Deputies.*

THE FIRST DEPUTY: Lambert de Besme!

LAMBERT: I am here.

THE FIRST DEPUTY: Lambert, in many respects we
 have been unfair to you.

THE SECOND DEPUTY: Yes, in many respects we have
 been unfair to you. It is true. I have always said
 so.

LAMBERT: Say what you have to say.

THE FIRST DEPUTY: I shall be frank with you. You
 have read the papers. The situation is serious.

LAMBERT: I know.

THE FIRST DEPUTY: Everything is going to pot. I
 came with these gentlemen. But in my opinion nothing can be done.
It is the Logic-of-things; we cannot contend with it.
And is it not just that each man should have his share
 of happiness!
But the truth of the matter is there's no more money.

LAMBERT: Bankruptcy already?

THE SECOND DEPUTY: It would be useless to conceal the
    facts. We have put up the shutters. Our credit is
    exhausted. Our liabilities are huge and cannot be
    discharged.

You are old in politics, and doubtless know the cause
    as well as we.

For where authority lacks, in its place one needs

The seduction of silver. The Government

Cannot meet its expenses. Tomorrow

Neither the clerks nor the army will be paid.

And as for the money borrowed, it is gone.

LAMBERT: What do you come to ask of me?

THE FIRST DEPUTY: Your counsel, Lambert.

LAMBERT: Here it is. The most certain plan is to de-
    camp.

THE FIRST DEPUTY: Do not jest, for you are en-
    dangered as well as we.

All authority comes from the common people.

And each year they set aside a fixed amount

For the task of government, that man may live in peace
    with his neighbour, and the cutthroat may not take
    his goods, and the roads may be maintained.

So a public fund is established, those that are weak
    submit, and levies, large and weighty, are paid the
    strong.

But each one wants to be ranked with the receivers,
    and the State does not meet its obligations.

Then it suspends payment. I should have preferred an
    earlier departure.

But if a syndic must be named, let him be chosen by us.
    We have selected you.
LAMBERT: And who are you?
THE THIRD DEPUTY: Don't you recognize me, Lambert? And these are bankers, merchants, and professors.
LAMBERT: I thank you, gentlemen. This step you have
    taken in regard to me, I admit it does me honour.
And first with regard to the interests of the public.
On these, like you, I do not waste a thought.
For this alone seems to you vital, immediate, pressing,—yourselves.
And as for you who come so generously to offer
The Government and the power, like a fund of insolency, I will not hide it from you,
I regard you as a pack of rogues; not one of you but
    is ready, while I defend you, to stab me in the back.
Yet know that if I accept
I shall not suffer advice nor brook remonstrance, but I
    shall do alone
That which shall seem to me opportune and good.
The laws shall not stop me, but like a physician, for
    such indeed is my trade,
(And I shall cure this country, I myself ill with its
    malady),
I shall act as the state of the case requires, and where it
    is best I shall use the knife.
And as for this that you call the "logic-of-things,"
Not being a coward or an imbecile, I do not know what
    it is.

43

The present moment alone is mine, and I have no wish
  to see beyond, but I shall act with wisdom and resolu-
  tion.
It is thus I shall save you and maintain the State.
Then regard this woman and turn yourselves towards
  her for all your fate is in her hands.
Answer, young girl, will you, or will you not, consent to
  be my wife?
For if she betroths herself to me, I live, and I shall do
  my labour and my task; and if
She rejects me my name shall be known among men no
  more.

                                        (*Pause*.

THE FIRST DEPUTY: Speak, young girl!
LALA: Coeuvre!

                                        (*Silence*.

Coeuvre, do you hear me?
COEUVRE: What do you want of me, young girl?
LALA: Will you abandon me thus?

                                        (*Silence*.

Why don't you answer? Why do you let me speak?
Why are you silent? Will you let me thus be enslaved
  before your eyes?
COEUVRE: Marry this man who loves you.
LALA: I do not love him. I will not marry him.
COEUVRE: You have promised.
LALA: I have promised? Well, I will not keep my
  promise.
I do not know what manner of man he is.
Look, all of you. Behold

44

The one at whose feet I cast myself.

> (*She casts herself at the feet of* COEUVRE.

Do not despise me, Coeuvre. See, I speak to you in the sight of everyone, and I have put my honour beneath your feet.

And behold I lie across your path and your foot has touched my head,

And will you not seek with your hands to discover who it is, and raise this shape that groans like one that is sorely wounded?

For perhaps you are like a man who, journeying at night, does not know that he has arrived,

And groping along the ground, he does not know what thing obstructs his feet.

—It is I.

Raise me then and hold me erect till I say to you, "Enough."

And do not release me till then, for fear I should lack the strength to stand unaided.

Have pity upon me, for why am I alone, having no brothers or kinsmen to succour my distress,

If not that I may be your chattel, stranger, and that I may belong to none but you.

> (*Silence.* COEUVRE *puts his foot on her back.*

Speak, Coeuvre.

COEUVRE: I reflect, my foot on your back.

LALA: Reply.

COEUVRE: Assuredly I regard you with no joy, thing prone upon the earth!

LALA: O Coeuvre, did you not say that you went along
the roads picking up pebbles and fallen bits of bark?
And I am worth more than a stick or a handful of
grass that one plucks.
COEUVRE: What restrains me from doing this? Once
more I feel the ancient woe return.
And I am like a physician who, on the way to his
wedding,
Encounters a sick man in his course, and takes him
home, and gives no heed to the waiting house of his
nuptials, filled with kinsmen and friends.
For all the joy of man is it not indeed, as the common
tongue reports,
Woman, that in possessing her he may be satisfied, and
that the male may have access to the female?
Be glad, my soul, be glad, Coeuvre, for you have found
your joy and placed your foot upon it.
This woman, is she not fair? And does she not say
she loves you? Seize and take!
For has she not two eyes and a mouth and hands
And hair that you may untwine,
And does she not put them all between your arms?
It is night. Since my eyes obscurely penetrate beyond
the length of my arm, I will believe my hands.
Who am I that I should covet another happiness, I,
scarcely more than thirty years of age? We shall
die and leave no memory behind.
Then arise, my joy! Be my wife.
LALA: Spread over me
This veil I have brought.

(They spread the veil over her. She rises.
I salute you, Coeuvre.

COEUVRE: I salute you in your veil.

But since I cannot see you I will weigh you. Certainly
you are heavy and of a goodly weight.

(He lifts her from the ground.

I can hardly raise your feet from the ground. Behold,
I take you for my charge.

See, you that stand about me, men and women,

And you, assemblage more antique, trees, roof of
branches, hither bend your eyes!

And you, O largest circle,

Firmament, and stars

But newly lighted in the high, white air,

As a man who sleeps in a farm-house at morning hears
above him only the wakening multitude of doves!

And thou, O hierophant,

Who on the brink that shall engulf thee standest with
uplifted torch!

I have taken this woman and such is my measure and
portion of the earth.

(He lifts her again.

I will weigh you, Sleep obscure!

Behold I approach this veil and grasp its gauzy mesh.
Take me with your sleep-bestowing hands.

For I needs must sleep that you may take my soul, and
that you may receive

My breath, and that I may have communication with
you.

(He approaches her and putting his hands on

*her shoulders, touches her cheek with his
cheek beneath the veil.*

I salute you, O my wife.

LALA: O Coeuvre, I am delivered to your hands.

COEUVRE: Remove your veil.

(*He puts aside her veil.*

O star of eve, is it you?

LALA (*in a low voice*): Hail, O Coeuvre!

COEUVRE: Let me breathe your scent which is like the
scent of earth,

When, gleaming, laved with water like a shrine, it produces blue and yellow flowers,

And like the scent of summer, perfuming the straw
and the grass, and like the scent of autumn.

And I hold you and possess you in the breath that enters my nostrils.

LALA: Let a bounteous ivy wreathe about my brow

With its wild clusters blending orange-flowers!

Because my life has not been lived in vain!

But like a fruit suspended between the leaves, you seize
me, gently pulling,

And I am in your hand,

At your mouth, and here is the branch to which I cling!

COEUVRE: Let me breathe your scent which is like the
scent of the earth.

There comes forth from you a breath, so strong that I
reel with it, like the reek of a grave, like the scent
of an open trench.

O woman! O female comrade! bitter friend!

O our bitter life, O love, like the bitter orange,

So suave to the scent, so bitter and strange to the heart
    and to the mouth!

                    (*They draw apart and remain silent.*

LAMBERT (*approaching*): Lala, let me salute you be-
    fore I go.

Farewell!

                    (*He kisses her on the shoulder.*

Farewell!

THE FIRST DEPUTY: Lambert, will you not let us have
    an answer?

LAMBERT: You have it.

THE FIRST DEPUTY: Will you return with us?

LAMBERT: No.

THE FIRST DEPUTY: I can assure you all necessary
    powers will be given into your hands.

LAMBERT: It is finished!

THE SECOND DELEGATE: Listen, nevertheless . . .

LAMBERT: It is finished!

THE FIRST DEPUTY: Have you so little regard for your
    country?

LAMBERT: I do not know.

Excuse me.

THE FIRST DEPUTY: What? Just because of that
    woman?

LAMBERT: Here a patch of forehead, there a beard,

The torch lights up a garment, gleams on hair or at-
    tentive eyes.

O, ye that are here!

Behold me like a man at the point of death,

Who, coming to himself, perceiving his kinsmen, who

surround him with their eyes, with his eyes demands in terror where he is.

Your faces appear to me sinister.

It is finished!

The illusion in which I have tried to live Is torn, and behold me miserable and bare among my enemies.

Receive me, earth, and let my name no longer be known among them!

But hearken, ye, and be my witnesses.

I deny you, O Joy!

I have said it. The word I bore within me has been proffered now at last. I deny you, O Joy!

It was in vain that I mixed with the public clamour. The word I wished to muffle cries aloud!

I deny you, O Joy, I divide myself from you, enjoyer of happiness!

And you, piercing dart, do not leave me, cherished Grief! Gush forth, water of tears! Humble earth, be my love and my bed!

O wound, I will consider thee.

Accept me, O ye whose dwelling is most low, living men that are seated among the dead!

O desolation, like a mother I will kiss you in the midst of your earthy visage!

(*He goes out.*

BESME: Farewell. See, the day is breaking.

As for me, I am going to bed. O that I might sleep!
(*He withdraws.*

THE FIRST DEPUTY: A day disturbed and charged with menaces.   Let us go.

                                        (They go out.

COEUVRE (*to* LALA):   You, come.

                                        (They go out.

Act Two

LAMBERT: I have no heart for toil, and I can
        scarcely pull
        My spade from the soil. Above me no bird sings,
    no bell in the distance chimes the call to prayer.
And yet I have scarcely lowered my eyes, I am forced
    to look on high.
A day of solemn augury has come. And I strain my
    eyes like a procession that gathers and falls into
    rank, without a word,
Before the profound cathedral gives it entrance.
The day once more!
Piercing the clouds a long ray of sunlight
Illuminates the city. I see the buildings and bel-
    fries reappearing, and the clustered roofs of the
    houses shine like gold. And already it is over.
What does it matter? Future and past do not exist
    for me.
But full of terror and reverence, I regard the earth
    and the sun,
And my care is, pressing it strongly with my foot, to
    bury the trenchant iron of the spade.

                    (*He resumes his work. Enter* LALA.

LALA: Lambert de Besme!

(*She throws a clod of earth at him.*

LAMBERT (*straightening up*): And who are you?

LALA: Lala!

I am Lala. Lala! It is I. Do you not recognize me?

LAMBERT: What do you come here to do?

LALA: And what are you doing in that grave yourself,
digger of graves?

LAMBERT: I am like the seamstress, stitching a bridal
robe,

Who works, all engrossed in her breadths, and like
the swallow that makes its nest with clay.

LALA: Lambert de Besme, I bring you news.

Inequality among men exists no more.

Men will no longer be poor, Lambert. There will
be no more poverty. For why

Should some have too much and others not enough?

But each shall receive his share, according to his need.

And never again shall the baby die at its mother's
dried-up breast,

But she, like the heifer that crops fresh grass, the milk
shall round her innocent breasts.

So come forth from this grave, come forth!

For I will love you yet, O my adopted father! Know
that I've left my husband and am free.

LAMBERT: You have left him?

LALA: Yes.

I have had a son by him.

LAMBERT: Go and take care of it!

LALA: Who is my son, and who is my husband,

When like the sheep in the sheep-fold as morning
  comes, smelling the nutritious grass, bleating,
Crowding against the doors,
I hear a living people raise its voice?
And I said to him, "Make yourself heard and cry
  aloud! Speak.
To the poor and to the rich! What black words that
  no one understands are you inscribing there?
Write for living men, and your strong words, borne
  aloft like a whirlwind, shall enter into them by the
  ears and by the nose!"
But he, like a man who looks instead of listening, with-
  out replying or baring his teeth, laughed.
And as our roads parted, I left him.
But you, come forth from that grave, come forth! For
  the table is set and all shall gather there in joy to
  partake of bread and wine, and none shall be turned
  away.
LAMBERT: And who will dig my graves? I am the
  labourer of death and not the guest of life.
LALA: Friend, think not of death, but of living!
For the living will establish among themselves
A city, and it shall have no statute-books,
But, like the bee in his cell, each man will make the law
  for himself.
LAMBERT: I know nothing of all this. Let me perform
  my task. Why do you come to seek me out again?
  I dwell in a more ancient city.
And from every side, through the streets of that other

city, encompassing us about, all smoking as if it
  burned,

Towards our gates the funeral processions mount each
  day. And I, I receive all comers. They enter, new
  arrivals in the city:

It has no laws and each for himself measures his portion there.

LALA: Come, and take pity on your brothers! Come,
  and I shall love you yet! Come and live!

  (*Enter* AVARE.

LALA: Well, what's new today?

AVARE: O Lala, there is nothing new but this: The
  strong spring is here!

Come out of the city and in your eyes will be mirrored
  the willow-blossoms and the colour of the earth that
  green grass pushes through.

Once as, standing beside a horse, in a ferry-boat, I
  crossed the harbour of New York,

I saw all the port with its boats and hills and the dis-
  tant line of the sea

Paint itself, violet-hued, in that large, snuff-coloured
  eye.

As for me, if you look between my lashes,

You will see a crowd that grows more dense and
  heaves,

Revealing faces only.

LALA: Certainly, though you keep silence, the crowd,
  when you appear, turns toward you. What is the
  latest news?

55

AVARE: The bell does not ring and the factory gates are
    shut.
  The fires are all cold and the engineer has slipped the
    belt from the wheel.
  The merchant has not taken down his shutters. Not a
    wheel turns in the gigantic streets.
  The city has retired from toil, the people with one ac-
    cord
  Resolve to stay quietly at home for a day or for two
    days;
  Nevertheless the year weeps and laughs like a young
    virgin and the sweet rain no sooner wets the pave-
    ment than it is dried again by a burst of sun.
LALA: For what do they wait?
AVARE: For me to speak to them.
  With vague mouths, the multitude awaits the form of
    the word.
  And such is the force of him who having, he alone,
    conceived the sterile crowd's inchoate thought, offers
    the Idea,
  And seeing what he wills, and willing with that which
    wills in it, does not hesitate to pronounce, "It must
    be done!"
  And, sharing the necessity of his own syllogism, stat-
    ing the principle imposes the conclusion.
LALA: What do you offer?
AVARE: This people bores itself.
  It takes no pleasure in its nourishment. Brandy and
    debauch have not consoled it.
  And I will explain the reason.

fragmentation

The workman of other days held all his work entire
between his hands,

And, as the sight of colour charms the heart,

Finding beauty in his work he enjoyed the work itself,

And, knowing the buyer, he had in view a precise re-
quirement.

But today all the grace of work has been done away
with, all its honour, and all its genius.

And man has no longer for end the satisfaction of another man, but supplies a general need,

And his work has no merit save utility, and machines
perform it for him.

Through this already two liberties are withdrawn,
choice in the means and order in the work,

And also I say that a double consent is refused,

Of the intelligence which, having the end in view, re-
solves on its attainment,

And of the will which, attaching itself to the work,
forgets the burden of toil.

And so, whatever his wage may be, the workman be-
comes a servile workman,

And, being a slave, he longs for liberty.

LALA: Will you give it to him?

AVARE: I shall make him understand his slavery.

(She laughs.

Why do you laugh?

LALA: What does it matter, Avare, to you and me?

Do you seek the happiness of the greatest number?

AVARE: He who plans to dislodge a mass from its sup-

ports, or to overthrow, having struck the proper
point, the obstacle of a thick and lofty wall,

It is needful that, having erected his machine, he should
industriously calculate its actions and the tension of
its springs.

O Lala, I have not embarked on a mediocre task.

Having taken stock of myself, observed my body and
seen my patient, strong, and docile will,

I have deemed the executive force was adequate and
that it would not be needful to find in another the
motive of the deed.

O Lala, Fable has spoken of kings and legislators who
go, in secret profound, to consult a nymph or a
prophetess,

Or that a sounding shell they apply to the ear instructs.

But each conceals in himself, more deeply hidden, a
more truthful oracle:

On the corner-stone of our nature resides the proposi-
tion of the spirit.

And with the greater part of men, conquered by sleep
and dream, it raises only a sigh, scarce audible, an
inefficacious voice,

But in me, as with the woman who in her womb feels
the stir of a male child, there lives

The word which has the ear itself for tongue, and, like
a captive, this

With propriety demands action and liberty;

So much so that it does not suffer either division in me
or the exterior obstacle, chaotic and inert.

LALA: You have explained very perfectly what you wish.

(*She laughs.*

AVARE: Why do you laugh?

LALA: Who can tell why I laugh or why I weep or smile?

How does it matter to you what is done by an unreasoning woman?

AVARE: What satisfaction have you given me? Do you think I could divide myself from you?

LALA: In truth, Avare, you have done ill to receive me into your home.

For I do not lie in your bed nor occupy myself with your nourishment and I have not even let you touch my hand.

Think that I did not enter by the door, but by the window, that doubtless you left open, like a wasp.

AVARE: What have you come to do in my home, young woman?

LALA: Floating like a tufted cotton-seed between the sea and the moon, no doubt the wind may have borne me thither.

Do not ask me what I have done, nor why I did it.

But the most severe will not regard me without a sign of content, and gaiety will penetrate him as with the little child that reflects before it smiles.

Nothing is so imprisoned that the youth of liberty may not prove itself the stronger; nothing is so sad that joy may not be more certain; nothing is so certain

59

that my presence may not improve it; I vanquish the
hardest heart, I dissolve the most enduring ties;

The voice of the bird one sees on the highest branch
at the same moment as the morning star, is so sweet
that one does not know whether indeed it sings,

Or one only sees the eternal star that shines upon its
heart.

The solitary man who, after a day of ploughing,
seated before his table suddenly hears the first strains
of the violin

Experiences so sudden a refreshment that the heart
fails him and the soul, halted upon itself,

Deliberates as in the dissolution of tears.

The sick man waking at evening, after a long and profound sleep,

Feels he is cured, and, turning his head to the left,

Toward the window shaded by thick, green branches
where sparrows gather and cheep, he sees in the
crimson sky that it is Easter!

In the same way I bring irresistible hope! And let no
one count on seizing me and installing me in his home

Like a cow that gently licks with its tongue the wall
to which it is shackled.

AVARE: Have you not married Coeuvre and had a son
by him?

LALA: Did I really marry him? Did I have a son by
him? I do not know. I remember it no more.

Coeuvre has no further need of me, and finds my ex-
altation vain in the glory he sublimely envisages; he
treads his way alone

60

Like a man who has at his left impenetrable shades and
at his right a wall that he follows, groping.

And you also, Avare, would you not desire to have satisfaction from me?

AVARE: Do not imagine you made me say

A thing unsuited to my gravity. Who can tell what
you feel or what you think? Why do you smile upon
me to refuse me?

LALA: Learn that there is a *no*

More joyous to him who hears it than a *yes!*

And as for my heart, it is that of a child at play;

And as for what I think, it is in my feet when I dance.

There is a dance for the day and for the hour, and at
times I stamp the earth

As if restrained by too strong a tie,

And there is the dance of the forest and of the river,
and I feign this strife, of striving

With the current that masters the drunkard, sweeping
him off his feet.

AVARE: Are you not woman even as the others are?

LALA: The woman is nearer the earth than the rest of
you. In closer proximity she breathes its fumes.

And thus it is that they say, in days of old,

The python's spirit filled her and the Prophetess of
thieves,

Two javelins in her hand, bespattered with blood from
a slaughtered ox, danced round the bonfire where the
cauldron boiled!

And, in like fashion, I, bending above this people all

61

astir, grow drunken with the scent of wine and dust
and the earthy grape that ferments,

And I shall make myself their prophetess, and the cry
of my mouth shall fill their souls with dread.

AVARE: Here is your husband, Lala, and here is Besme.

(Enter COEUVRE *and* BESME.

LAMBERT: And here is Lambert who takes his stand beside you.

*(He comes out of the pit he is digging and
stands erect, some distance away.*

BESME: I salute you, Avare. A singular meeting-place!

(He sniffs the air with a constrained smile.

AVARE: Certainly these are not your gardens and reservoirs. This is a different garden.

And it is the place I have chosen for rendezvous

Since this peace has been established.—Listen, no
sound mounts towards us from the City.

It is fitting that, our feet on this dead flesh, we discuss
affairs of the flesh that is alive.

BESME: What a frightful odour of decay! The dead
body in the depths of the earth grows aware of the
ancient spring

And stretching its bones, it turns upon its side.

(He seems distraught.

AVARE: What have you to say to me?

BESME: Avare,

For this vague multitude, prey of the wind, has in you
the head that sees,

Sniffs, listens, thinks, decides,

Explain to me what is happening today.

62

Up to now has not labour been a thing of the market-
  place that one man buys and that another sells,
So that the only matter of debate has been the de-
  termination of the price?
But today I do not know what these people want; they
  formulate no demands,
But, as if attainted with stupidity, at the same moment
  all
Lay down their tools and abandon their machines.
What do you ask? Speak, that we may reply,
And do not keep the silence of the brute.

AVARE: There is the rub. And if it pleases us to answer
  nothing at all?

BESME: Do you think you can live without eating? Do
  you think you can eat without working?

AVARE: Besme, our bread is baked.

BESME: Come and take it. You will find the crust is
  hard.

(*Silence.*

AVARE: Why should you not perish?
  You have no desire to live.

BESME: What do you mean?

AVARE: I know you and I have lived among you.
  No one speaks but that in his eyes
  You may read how bored he is with the reply that he
    is going to hear, and his voice interrupts blank noth-
    ingness.
  A bat flits through your salons.
  In the theatres you accumulate about the central light
    like butterflies that have for body a worm.

Each organism that does not perform its function putre-
fies.

All putrefaction produces emptiness. Each empty
thing that lives but in the shell crumbles with its own
weight at the first touch of the wind.

Thus the hand with which we have seized you finds in
you an obscure assent.

The leaf is not so well attached to the twig but that it
yellows, and when his time has come peacefully the
insect turns over on his back.

LAMBERT (*advancing*): Speak, what have you to answer, brother?

BESME: Lambert!

LAMBERT: I salute you, Besme, in my dwelling: enter!
Above the city the pollen of your trees comes to impregnate mine.

BESME: What are you doing in this place?

LAMBERT: I have charge of opening
The door of the return, which those who encounter it
do not recognise, inert and deaf,
This threshold man crosses clothed in a garment of
wood.

BESME: You have chosen such a life?

LAMBERT: I have faced the truth and made myself the
equal of the dead.
But come, speak! Reply to what Avare has said.

BESME: What would you have me reply?

LAMBERT: You do not know, my brother? Then I will
question you and you shall answer me.
What do you come to demand of this people?

Besme: I come towards this people with lazy hands as towards an obstructed waterfall,
And I demand its work.
Lambert: And why do you wish it to work?
Besme: That it may eat.
Lambert: And that it may eat in order to work?
Besme: Does not every force have its function?
Lambert: Does not every function have its end?
Besme: The end of the work is the product and the end of the product is exchange.
Lambert: And it is, in short, an exchange you propose, extending one hand and with the other unclosing the door of the safe, profound and black.
The labourer tilled his field, eating his rye and bacon and clothing himself with his flax.
The artisan worked at his bench and, weaver, he knew each day the length of cloth his loom could produce and he knew the value thereof, according to the dimensions of his elbow.
At this juncture you appeared.
And to the labourer, dependent for his bread on the rain and the sun, and to the artisan
Who, like the anxious spider, watched his precarious prey,
You offered on the one hand the security of a wage,
On the other, a handful of sous no longer gave the choice only between one merchant and another;
But the round piece you put in his hand conferred
A lien on the world entire;

And the vast world was put in a lottery. You gave
   out a ticket.

And it was thus you procured

The work you needed, forming these cities.

Correct me if I deceive myself. But I speak of things
   indubitable and certain.

BESME: Have we deceived you?

A valuation has been put on man.

And he lives alone no more, but has communion with
   the whole universe of things and men.

LAMBERT: You have not deceived us.

There is nothing you have proposed with which we
   would not have seduced ourselves.

The double good that you promise us, you have it
   yourself between your hands.

And the first is insurance against inquietude, the un-
   binding of the obligation of toil.

BESME: Each man must work, the poor man for the
   rich, the rich man for the poor.

LAMBERT: Then reply to the question I asked you a moment since: Why? All effort that has desire for
   motive supposes satisfaction for its end.

All satisfaction is individual, each end is fixed and de-
   termined.

—And the second good is the consummation of pleasure; seated, you own the world like a loaf of bread.

And such in your closed hand is the gold that pays and
   buys.

BESME: So be it.

LAMBERT: And now, O brother, regard the people that

lives beneath your yoke and the structure and division of our society.

Observe the employee at his office, the labourer at his job, the merchant at his counter, the student at his book,

Consider the society comprising all mankind like a devil-fish glued against the ball of the world,

Enlacing it with its myriad supple arms, a body of pumps set with retractile suckers,

And you, O rich man, as though in the midst of the beast which tastes in its heart and understands in the secret depths of its stomach.

See the bodies that pass in thousands through factory doors, to the shrieking of the whistles, see the poor, see the women and children, count the cattle.

Count the heads devoid of name and bare of honour, that are born and live and die as though plagued by a perpetual December,

In poverty, in ignorance, in vice, and in servitude.

And sniff, none the less this lives!

Suppose that one of these beings who have spent their lives in your hand turns towards you all at once as an old man,

And that, considering you, with the decrepit nodding of his head,

Lifting his trembling hand to your mouth, he holds it open with two wasted fingers.

What will you reply to his interrogation?

BESME: Death annuls the fastenings of the lower jaw,

The part that speaks and eats, and dissevering itself
from its supports, beneath the holes of the ears,
It separates from the skull.
And such is the response the row of my teeth will make
if he inserts his fingers in my mouth, obscure and
moist.
That is if I do not bite him.
Is not the belly filled, in the fold of its intestines,
Whether you give it soup and potatoes to digest,
Or the most tender bread and choicest meat?
Is drunkenness a different thing whether we sip cham-
pagne
Or, standing at the bar, two cabbies gulp from a great
bowl of crude and bitter wine?
If we have the cakes, have you not the appetite, the
enjoyment, have you not the desire?   All things are
equivalent.
And as for liberty, I tell you truth.
No bondage is insupportable, no man is tied with too
short a cord,
Provided that in the midst of his brothers he applies
his heart to a daily task, and to an assiduous toil.
Woe to him who lives by himself, apart from other
men; like a labourer discharged, with idle hands, he
wanders near his former working-place.
LAMBERT: Answer, what is the message that you bring?
You that have this liberty, who can hold your visage
raised, what is it that you see?
BESME: The extent of space, the duration of time.
I, the great Besme, I speak:

The weariness of death is like the solitude I envisage.
                            (LAMBERT *bows his head.*

Since you have forced me to speak, learn my reply, and understand it if you have the power.

Salt and poison impregnate all the earth. The more this world is fair, when it laughs in the freshness of its leaves,

The more I savour the futile poignancy, the utter mockery of being here. I have known all things and the hesitation of death is comparable to my dissatisfaction.

            (LAMBERT *remains silent, with bowed head.*

LALA: It is well, Lambert. Come. It is enough!

Another duty than that of answering devolves upon you now.

LAMBERT: What did you say?

LALA: Do you not understand what now impends? Depart, for it is not fitting that this thing should happen in your sight.

LAMBERT: For the last time I look upon your face.

LALA: Gaze at it then. O my adopted father, do you now understand the reason I refused you till this hour?

So strong is the young girl's face that the young man forgets his master and his father.

But it was fitting, friend, that mine should have been reserved to undo a knot more close and more profound.

Irremediable, O Lambert, is your liberty.

Why busy yourself with the liberty of others when this
has been granted to you?

> (LAMBERT *slowly moves away and is seen to
> sink down behind a tomb.*

AVARE: What has happened?

LALA: Pay no attention to it. Lambert is dead.

> (*Silence.*

And you, what do you say, Coeuvre? Are you not
happy to find your wife again?

COEUVRE (*looking at her as if he were trying to recognize her*): Who are you? I no longer know you.
Of what use is the tuft and the tail of hair that grows
behind your head,

If not that a fist invisible to your eyes, twisted in it,
may conduct you elsewhere?

LALA: Will you lie, and say that I did not cause you
pain?

COEUVRE: So be it.

It is true, the glory of my youth is gone, and you bore
it away with you.

Peace in the sunlight, the sudden surprise of flowers
wherewith I saw myself decked has perished now.
Despoiled I leave your hands.

But I myself remain, and, black and bare, I meditate
new branching, other flowers, and the heaviness of
fruit.

LALA: Behold, O Coeuvre, I am no longer with you!

The door that I have opened to go out has filled your
room with moonlight.

Yet, confess, was I not worthy to be loved?

Will you not accuse me of having lied to you? Do you
surely know what I have taken from you?
I have transferred it to Avare. I share his lodgings
now.
And as for the duty to still remain with you, have I not
borne you a son?
Thus all is over between us twain, O Coeuvre!
And if you ask the reason, I shall not answer you.

COEUVRE: So be it, Lala.

LALA: How does it happen I meet you in company with
this man?
Tallow and sugar, Coeuvre,
Flour, timber, blended coffees, oils, and gold,
Are not the matter of your speculation, that I see you
maintain with your arms the heavy cask that crushes
you.
But since Lambert has withdrawn, since I find myself
before you, and Avare disdains to speak,
It is I who will explain his error to this Prince of those
that eat.
Besme, the most succulent meats, the choicest wines,
The possession of gems, these are not qualified to
nourish or to kindle in the soul
The inner light of wisdom.
But as the body discovers and abstracts
In matter the elements that are proper to it,
So the human essence finds in its like alone
The merited order of its satisfaction.
But the alliance and marriage a man concludes with
a woman

Are insufficient and, like friendship, love too exhausts itself.

As one note contains the series without end and its harmonies to the full extent of the two limits of hearing,

Each man, to live with all his soul, claims multiple accords. And,

If he be not dung or filth for which science does not know a profitable use,

I think there is no being, however debased and vile,

But is needful for our unanimity.

Let nothing human be alien to our pleasure, and let the law be ascertained through whose changeless operation

No man can escape an invincible harmony,

And let nothing be lost or vain! And such is the city that we shall constitute.

Isn't this worth striving for, and haven't I spoken well?

COEUVRE: You have spoken well, Lala.

LALA (*smiling*): Since we had power to tame the heart of fire and the thunderbolt, constraining them to toil,

Who can doubt that we shall find the way to spread a snare so infinite

That none can escape the total harmony?

And as each definite object has its dimensions and weight,

Even so on the one hand man has tasks, and on the other hand, his function.

And such is the equilibrium he maintains, here main-
taining himself;

Such is the social unity, such is the principle of exchange.

Understand, O Besme, in what consists the reality
of exchange, and do not let yourself be fooled by
symbols.

As gold is the symbol of merchandise, so merchandise
is itself a symbol,

Of the need that calls it forth, of the effort that creates
it,

And what you name exchange, I call communion.

BESME: Conclude, finish.

LALA: The city is the form of humanity.

O what will be the order, what the ineffable peace,
of the city of mankind,

When, the value of the symbol having been restored
again, each individual will at once attain an immediate relation with his fellows,

And by his position having learned his needs, once
knowing them he will not exceed the measure,

And in pure liberty will repay the equivalent of that
which he has taken,

If freedom is only in necessity.

The world has been delivered to man by knowledge
and now to each man all men are given, and only the
integral humanity is constituted as a body is,

In the architecture of its members and in the function
of its organs,

In the plenitude of justice, in the potency of life and in unshakable solidarity.

COEUVRE: Well spoken.

LALA: Then come with us, Coeuvre, and range yourself beside Avare and me,

That, having demolished this city,

We may use the beams and stones for making something new.

COEUVRE: No.

LALA: Are you satisfied, then, with that which now exists?

COEUVRE: I could never follow out to the end the reflection necessary to find if I am satisfied, yes or no.

I am content to observe what now exists.

For nothing could or can

Have being, which is not at this very moment: all things for me are present.

I establish, I assist; but no more than I attempt with my fingers to force the opening of a bud,

Or to rifle the womb of the mother to hale therefrom her fruit, if you demand

That in my proper person I put my hand to the work, that I direct these forces the eternal flux of which I contemplate, and propound my own idea,

Thought fails me and my heart, distraught, refuses to understand.

But be certain of this, O woman, that if I saw a house about to fall on the heads of its occupants,

Only after the length and trouble of reflection would I ask its owner to examine it.

But how can the rest of you have so little sense of
music as to utter, unconstrained, a cry out of measure
and accord?

And how great is your impudence and audacity, not
having the principal charge, when you lay your hand
on a thing

Which is sacred insomuch as it exists, how swollen is
your folly

To think you can build a finer edifice, using human
souls like bricks

And like beams of which one has figured the torque
and stress!

LALA: Well then, Avare,

For you alone have the right to speak and pronounce,
Avare,

Make known your reply, and hearken to what they say
to you.

Regard the human extent in the peace of noon and,
clear and white, behold the form of the city

That has received the stone and the cement laid down
in these ancient fields.

By the effect of the clouds that cross the immense and
open sky

As the shade of a tree extends above the City.

Since from the place where we are, one does not see the
filth and ordure,

Forget the wrong and anguish, let your genius conquer
by tranquillity.

Listen to Coeuvre's advice.   Maintain what is.

Think of the arduous labour of the past through which
    it has unfolded like a flower,
Unclosing the design of voids and fissures like a legible
    inscription.
Have pity on the ancient City. Stay your destroying
    hand
Even as a pious and compassionate man
Will not overthrow an ancient wall in May, for fear
    of crushing the nests where the swallow feeds her
    tender brood,
Fear to strike at life, fear the unction of blood and the
    tears of those in whom there is no fault.
Why act through yourself? Entrust your thought
    to time, and it will not be vain. Time will execute
    it like a workman who scrupulously follows each de-
    tail.
AVARE: Besme, Coeuvre, Lala,
    If I can change my face for another and if I can come
    forth from my carapace of ribs,
I can as easily change my heart and my decision.
Let others incline their ears and bind themselves to
    maintain with "Necessity" an imperturbable accord;
As for me, I contain it in myself and in my spirit it finds
    its support and its proposition.
Like a hatching eagle my head shall burst its shell!
Why should you be astonished and why are you filled
    with dread?
If the firm earth shakes in the thickness of its mass,
If the suture of the sky flaps in a thunder-clap, if the
    Ocean, swept by equinoctial gales,

Uproots its capes and like casks rolls its commingled
isles,

Why should you be amazed that this human ocean, this
sea of souls and blood,

One fine morning should begin to boil, and should burst
the encircling wall

Of the reservoirs wherein you would contain it, when
the hour has come and Mars enters into the Lion?

And birth is also a sign, birth of such men as he who
stands before you, Avare.

BESME: What do you think you can do?

AVARE: I do not *think* as you think. I suppose, Besme,

That you have tamed your heart and drive it where
you will, like the herbivorous ox

That a child conducts by the straight, integral way.

As for me, I have made it my master, and I listen to its
voice

As to that of an old, blind man, endowed with inexplicable wisdom.

It is ancient in my breast and since the beginning of
man, placed under my fifth rib, this continues the
beating of the undying heart.

Origin and chief, profoundly it digests the nourishment
drawn from the senses and the brain,

And, as the hour strikes when the tooth of the year
enmeshes,

Decision is its sphere, with the putting in operation,
and our will

Cadences on its movement.

It is in us and we are in it as well, for with every
    respiration it receives us
Entire in its cavity, and drives us forth again.
And so I have secretly made myself this vow.
To deliver in myself this thing through which I am one.
I shall not die without knowing liberty.

BESME: So all is finished?

AVARE: Hark.

    *(Songs, cries, in the distance. One hears the
        uproar of a crowd on the march.*

Hark to the elocution of the crowd like the sputtering
    of frying grease.

    *(A gust of wind drives over them the dust and
        smoke of the City.*

For the last time breathe the odour of the city, expand
    your nostrils o'er the human mass,
Sense the odour of the flesh beneath the garments, the
    cooking of food, the sweat of men and machines, the
    dust that mounts 'neath the stirring of innumerable
    feet.
All is finished.
The volume of a completer smoke shall rise from the
    opening, like an open vase, from the orifice of the
    City.
As the man who arrives at the height of a thunder-
    storm
Discovers, turning back to the gulf from which he has
    emerged, no more than an opaque mist,
And in the other direction finds another.

                      (He goes out.

LALA: Farewell, Coeuvre, farewell, Besme.

(*To* COEUVRE.

Farewell, Coeuvre.

(*Pause.*

Farewell, Besme!

(*Pause. She goes out.*

BESME: I fear only the physical pain;
The strangling hands compressed about the throat,
the impact of the stone against the skull, the knee
on the stomach, the knife-thrust in the belly, the
crushing, the dislocated arm that snaps.
But if I question as to death itself I find in my soul
only a vague silence.
—Whence come these infantile tears?

COEUVRE: You weep, Besme?

BESME: What is happening? What is this that weeps
in me? I cannot repress this pang.
It is bitter, inconsolable. Should I have been unhappy,
then?

COEUVRE: You weep, Besme!

BESME: Had I then a right to be loved? What is this
wrong that has been done to me?
What is this? Heart wise and stern, is it you that
weeps?

COEUVRE: O Besme, let them flow, these solemn tears.

BESME: Ineffable suavity!
It is sweet to discover that another being places in you
his joy and his surprise.

COEUVRE: Bewail yourself, wounded heart!

BESME: Through knowledge I am placed outside of knowledge;

Through intelligence debarred from the comprehension of men.

COEUVRE: Have you never been in love?

BESME: If a woman had loved me my pain would not be less.

There is no one that understands me. No one knows this at the bottom of myself that even I do not know.

—Peace to this hour! Enough!

O Coeuvre, receive my last words.

COEUVRE: I am listening.

BESME: I have profoundly considered the nature of things, studying all their energies and virtues.

I it was who completing the imperfect force, supplying by my art the missing member,

Through many ingenious inventions eased the servile burden of man.

Through which, for having delivered him to the curse of dreams, I perish.

All my life I have busied myself with linking cause to cause, but my thought was not satisfied.

And it was only some months ago that I made this discovery

For not consummating which no doubt it is fitting that I die.

I have found ignorance again! O Coeuvre, although your spirit is great, poet,

I do not know if you can grasp what I am about to

say: there is a knowledge underlying knowledge and we shall call it Ignorance.

COEUVRE: Instruct me in it, O Besme.

BESME: All things are inexplicable. And what is this insatiate hunger consuming the soul of knowledge

But the appetite to exhaust that which is not essential?

Each thing exists in its difference, and is based, individual, on an incommunicable principle.

Where you see Causes and Laws (exalting the capital letter like an idol)

I only find the working of a machine. There is no necessity except the logic

Comprised in the ascertaining of the thing; all manner of explanation

Only makes the definition dilate; image abstract of the deed.

I designate Nothingness the foundation of all things, escaping with totality the capacity of our spirit. And that is why,

Made familiar with the commerce of energies profound,

I had planned to substitute for knowledge contact, to surprise the Being in its operation, contriving such a snare.

I blend this thought with Death's obscurity.

COEUVRE: Why do you think you will die?

BESME: I shall not escape my fate. It is fitting that I should perish, torn by the hands of the mob.

I wish, Coeuvre, at this moment supreme, like the very secret itself, to place in your hand this.

(*He detaches a stone from the ring he wears on his finger.*

As the freshness, they say, of the emerald, clear and green,

Revives a languishing spirit and insinuates gaiety,

It is thus that, in hours of fatigue and of confusion, taking between my fingers this jewel,

Where Pureness itself condenses to azure, and azure in turn to Night,

I began the consideration of ecstasy.

O Coeuvre, I give you this sapphire.

This limpid atom is all I have torn from my mines and excavations.   Receive

This drop of abstract night, pupil of primordial blindness.

And if you know how to place this stone beneath the fire of the lamp, or in the light of the moon,

Blue, you will see it flame between your fingers with six equal rays.

(*He gives him the stone.*

Farewell, Coeuvre.

(*He goes out.*

(*Muffled uproar off stage.   Very long pause.*

COEUVRE (*as if lost in a dream*):   . . . the thing.   It is here . . .

(*Long pause.*

The thing.   (*He shivers.*)   I am cold!   The wind is rising.   This grey sky!

(*He goes out.*

(*Clamour of an approaching crowd.   Above a*

wall at the back one sees pass across the stage flags, the barrels of guns, and BESME'S *head stuck on a bayonet.*
The sun sets in a confused sky.

Act Three

The ruins of the City.

GÉRIN: The sun that disappears midst the effusion of more blood,
    Does not devastate the City of the Clouds with a hole and a ruin more frightful
Than the human City that crashes to the ground in the consummation of dreams.
Like a leaf of parchment devoured by crawling flame,
Thus for ten days and nights, beneath the pitiless wind, in the fire that flames and snores,
Mountain of smoke in the sun, vivid splendour in the dark,
It has been consumed entire.
THYRSÉE: Such was the end. And the master of this land, Avare, who holds the heart of it between his legs, like a horse,
    Ordered that guards should be placed round that enormous pyre,
And that for the length of a year no desecrating foot
Should violate the majesty of the tomb, derange the completion of death.
And in the place of the multitude there is peace.
GÉRIN: On the date of the anniversary, having arisen again, we appear above the enclosure.

THYRSÉE: It does not become us, O Gérin, to recall these fourteen years
   Otherwise than by silence which joins the bones of the jaws, and the lips, and the lids of the eyes.
   Envisaging humanity on the day of its final effort, on the day of its definitive disaster, it is not fitting that such men as we
   Should break the silence otherwise than with a pitiful and humbled heart.
   You have seen it, Gérin, and how like the earth at the first day of the Creation, quivering beneath the breath of Chaos,
   It wished to constitute happiness in the image of a City!
   This is a song like the crackling of icicles, like the cry of stones to lime in the kiln,
   Uproar, sharp-edged to the ears of the gods, like that of the baby, who goes *ee, ee,* knowing no more than this,
   As if, with the curb of the alphabet removed, from the incoherent mouth emerged the form of a vow!
   But, the individual once uncurbed, what share of his own was so large but that of his neighbour seemed better in his sight?
   The moderation of order has prevailed and the authority of force.
GÉRIN: Ignorance, Thyrsée. . . .
THYRSÉE: You pronounce it;
   As it lives, there is not a pound of the flesh of man that does not think,

But impenetrable Nature with the matter of which he
is made has compelled him to share its blindness.

Not knowing what he is, how should he know what he
wishes? Now it is well, all is ended.

When in the flame of the thunderbolt the ocean like a
head

Comes to strike with the horn its bound till full ten
leagues away one hears the stone resounding like a
drum,

One would think the abyss was rising, that, flooding
the land again,

It would scour it like a raft and take for spoil

A harvest of straw, the dunghill blent with the cities
of human beings;

But in the morning who will not smile to see it more
blue than black, while the pure East has the hue of a
robin's egg and the pollen of the poplar,

And far off one sees the volcanoes smoke in the limpidity of the salty air!

GÉRIN: I salute the aerial immensity. I salute the expanse agleam!

I salute the sweet morn, I salute the Spring that waketh
all things new.

The chestnut-tree has burst the prisoning asphalt;

Free, nuptial, bathed with the roses of the night it
shakes its plumes and flowers coloured like the flesh
of an infant.

The water and the ardour of heaven have cleansed the
latrines and theatres.

And as for these millions of bodies, of men, of horses,
of dogs,

The flame of the conflagrations has consumed them,
and as for the flesh that remained,

The autumn and winter rains, the sun of May, of June,
of July, of August, of September,

Destroyed it, and, in accordance with the movement
of the planets,

It has dissolved into primitive elements, leaving these
bare bones,

Like dry and healthful boulders, amid the abundant
grass.

A clear, sweet water flows through the open sewers,
bordered with buttercups and mint.

It seems to me good and legitimate to live.   In nothing
I contest the veracity of light.

I thrust my hand in my mouth, and, exalting it midst
this heaven so pure and new,

I make this sacrifice of saliva!

> (AVARE *and* IVORS, *followed by the officers of
> the State*.

THYRSÉE (*to* GÉRIN):   There he is.   Take care not to
stare at him.   He does not like to be observed.

AVARE: I salute you, gentlemen.

GÉRIN: Greetings, Avare.

> (*Pause*.

AVARE: Hmm!   What a change is here!

> (*He stands for a long time with his eyes fixed
> upon the City in a mute consideration, then he*

*begins to laugh silently. Suddenly turning
about, he exclaims.*

Why do you look at me so?

THYRSÉE: We are not looking at you.

(AVARE *points towards a district of the City.*

GÉRIN: I recognize the gardens of Besme.

The quarters below are no more than a mass of wreckage.

AVARE: Surely I shall not hide it from myself, I am
satisfied.

O City!

For long, among the multitude, like a man that is swallowed up,

Wandering, lost and proscribed, in that place of scorn,
I have knocked the pavements with a heavy shoe.

And, both hands against the windows, I watched the
imprisoned fire in the centre of the stores.

I have set free the inner fire!

And now my task is done and thou, O City, like something old thou losest thy stones.

Ah, ah, I kiss thee, O breeze!

These falling planks, these twisted beams, it is the ruin
of my dungeon cell, it is the wound in the wall of the
door!

I see! Because of this my heart exalts itself like a
throne.

Truly, this hour is good!

IVORS: Avare, what are your wishes?

AVARE: O City!

IVORS: Speak, for our trust is in you.

AVARE: Trouble me not. I see, and I cannot glut my
gaze. I have destroyed you, City!
IVORS: When all men join together they possess
No more rights than one alone.

(*Pause.*

AVARE: It was when I had been wounded. I dreamed
a dream one night when there was snow.
Yes, the eve of Saint-Nicolas.
I tell you I saw myself sleeping on the ground, and it
was I know not where, beside the sea and its noise
like that of a browsing cow.
It was I indeed and I saw myself. And I was tormented
with many cares, such as those of a general in war,
For he needs a mind alert, like a man that is menaced
by death,
And as, half-swooning, I could not find how to finish
the thought that filled my mind,
I heard a voice from vacant depths of space, like one
Who, asleep by the couch of a patient, hears a sigh and
awakes: Avare, my name.
And I wished to answer, cry,
And mount the terrible horse to sweep mankind before
me,
As when one disembowels cities like ant-hills beneath
the spade!
But I was heavy as iron and remained upon the ground,
not uttering a word.
Again: Avare! And then for the third time:
Avare! Like syllables formed by a non-sonorous
mouth.

—What does this signify? What soothsayer has the
skill to explore the enigma with appraising thumb?
(*To* IVORS.

What do you say, my son?

IVORS: I can venture no opinion.

AVARE: The end. I shall sleep with Sesostris. I pass
with bygone things.

Then farewell, I depart. I leave this place forever.

GÉRIN: What did you say? What! You are not plan-
ning to go away, Avare?

You who have led us so far, you surely do not intend to
forsake us all at once.

THYRSÉE: Without another word, like people on whom
one turns one's back.

AVARE: What I have promised you I have fulfilled. I
have guarded your wives and children.

And I have established you in the solidity of peace,
making the wise man prevail by force.

Now remain united, like the tenets of a doctrine, like
a man beneath his skin.

Listen, Gérin, Thyrsée, and you, my son, Ivors!

Do not remember Avare, he is no more.—

Let respect find entrance to your ferocious souls!

Learn that justice is not separable from knowledge.
And if it pleases you

To put gold on the head of this young man, so be it!
(*He regards* IVORS *affectionately.*

You have seen these years. Let none of you, nevertheless, become so lost that he suffers the seduction

Of the changing voice of the negligible man.
—Out, that is my cry.

GÉRIN: Where do you cast your regard?

AVARE: Malediction on man!
And on all the works of man!
Because he creates falsehood.
Walling up his eyes with that which is not.
And I, I have destroyed it beneath my feet. At least
May this devastation have authority, and may this
   stinking endure!

GÉRIN: Avare, do not go!

THYRSÉE: What madness!

IVORS: Do not go. Remain with us!

AVARE: In the beginning I loved to be free.
And also I thought things existed there that were not
   to be despised:
The embracing of the well-beloved, like a combat with
   a swan!
The joy of acting bravely and of knowing, and of hold-
   ing and conducting with stalwart hands,
Or repose in the bounteous autumn, between the wife
   and the child.
But all of this is effaced and only the first desire en-
   dures.
That is why I forsake the sword.

> (*He unclasps it.*

Take it, Ivors! I resign it to your hands.
—Farewell. With nothing that lives do I wish com-
   munity.

91

No more than a virgin unicorn will I suffer the weight
   of a hand.
I aspire to tranquillity.
I will remain no more.   There where the voice may
   be heard anew,
It is there that I will go.   Edge of the tarn or trench
   beneath the beech-trees where the Bearers-of-seeds,
   with their knotted sarplers,
Have parted, treading diverging roads.

> (*He moves away.*

IVORS: Avare!
GÉRIN: Do you thus depart?   All alone, do you yield
   yourself thus . . .

> (AVARE *goes.*

He has gone!
THYRSÉE: You remain, Ivors.
   What have we learned in these years of search and
      tumult,
   If not that the Government's sacred head and the pri-
      mal motive force
   Must be taken from the control of changing factions
      and the curiosity of ignorant hands;
   And seeking where to seek it, we have found no re-
      treat more secret
   Than the heart of a man who above all men may be
      One.
   Be then over us, Ivors, the Prince.
GÉRIN: We salute you, Ivors!
ALL: Ivors!
IVORS: Why have you chosen me from all the others?

92

THYRSÉE: Why do you ask when you know well the answer? O young man, your face bears the seal of the Sun!

GÉRIN: What Avare has willed it behooves us to respect.

IVORS: Friends, that your words assail my ears with a sound amazing, or unexpected,

I could not say with any tinge of truth.

So be it.

My head, I confess, is ready for the crown.

Many men in the simplicity of childhood have their hearts touched by love, or like my father, the great Coeuvre, at times,

By the mystery of Wisdom, and the verbiage divine of Poesy.

As for me I have always felt a choice upon me, and with me a prerogative.

No passion blinds me, no pride has made me deaf.

But reckoning that equilibrium is the supreme good, it has seemed to me

That the government of the world is not too much for my soul to undertake.

So I shall be, if such is your will, above you, the Master,

Not as one who controls a dead man's goods or who exploits a field,

But above free men the master who ordains, who teaches and who judges,

With a tender solicitude

And an unimpeachable authority.

But first of all, for a certain doubt assails me, answer
me; what is the function of the Prince?

THYRSÉE: To administer to the nations happiness.

IVORS: And what is this happiness?

GÉRIN: A more certain security, a larger satisfaction.
                                                    (*Silence.*

THYRSÉE: Well, isn't that your opinion also?
                              (IVORS *remains with bowed head.*

GÉRIN: Have you anything different to suggest?
                                                    (*Pause.*

IVORS: No.

What, indeed, should be the function of the Prince if
not the assuring of happiness to his people?
                                                    (*Pause.*

O Gérin, and you, Thyrsée,

Is this, then, all the lesson you have gleaned from these
violent years

Like the inquietude and the rages of a lost soul that
seeks?

Have you so ill understood the lesson developed before
you

From argument to conclusion?   What, still the old
idea of happiness in enjoyment?

The multitude in itself does not contain its goal, its
happiness

Lies not in the quest of ultimate purposes but in the
wholesome exercise of its subordinate function.   Order

Is found in sacrifice, and it is needful that sacrifice be
esteemed and glorified.

I wish to be a conductor of men, not a shepherd of
browsing beasts.

THYRSÉE: Then will the end be found in the person
august of the Prince?

IVORS: No more there than in the people. The Prince
has his rôle as well: the Prince is not the principle.

No human being, no object that is caused,

Confines the virtue of the ultimate end.

And since no man may boast of its possession, in what
way could the society of men reveal its character,

Being only a means itself?

But it is here that the probe of my spirit halts. I hesitate.

GÉRIN: What is this procession?

> (*Enter* COEUVRE *wearing the insignia of a
> bishop and followed by the clergy.*
>
> *Silence.* IVORS *and* COEUVRE *gaze at each
> other fixedly.*

COEUVRE: Ivors!

IVORS: That is my name.

COEUVRE: You have grown since I left you, son of the
separation?

IVORS: What is this name you call me by?

COEUVRE: O child of my flesh, your birth was not the
consummation of two in one!

But two beings, charged with destinies by you,

Being doubtless freed from what they had in common,
have taken different paths.

IVORS: Man, are you my father, the great Coeuvre?

COEUVRE: I am.

IVORS: Let me then, O my father, at last consider you
and envisage my origin.

You are not unknown to me.   Surely the name of
Coeuvre will not be lost in the cycle of the ages,

Like a bell in the place impenetrable, like the accents
of the voice of the male.

No bell is comparable to that but the bell wherein all
sound reverberates beneath the single blow.

The astounded heart that hears it makes one no longer
aware which way to go, nor what return thus holds
our step suspended.

He who seeks old measures finds no familiar landmarks
in your verse;

It is not a road that conducts him, it is a sword that pro-
pels, it is a torch in the night that goes before!

The sound of words and their sense, dissolved in a
common phrase,

Have such subtle changes, such profound accords, that
the soul, recoiling on the intelligence,

Perceives that pure reason will not disallow a touch
delectable.

Such are the nuptials, O Coeuvre, to which you summon
us.

But now, O my father, explain this fatal silence, and
what obscure design

Made you refuse to men the communication of your
spirit.

COEUVRE: The child, O my son, with pure joy prattles
and plays; indiscreet, devoid of shame,

Like a bird that publishes abroad his glee,

But the man who has conceived love, or he who nourishes in his heart a secret supreme,

Pursues an opposite course and you behold him slowly
reduced to silence.

Without master and without example, placed in the
midst of the world like Adam between the rivers of
Paradise,

I loved it for the joy I encountered there.

But in the second stage of life, the embrace succeeded
the kiss,

Complaisance yielded to application, giving way to a
passion like the thirst for knowledge, and like the
sexual throe,

And I understood the harmony of things in their se-
quence and accord

And at last, having made the great discovery, in the
comprehension of unity and of the subtleties of difference I found the height of joy.

A pure eye and a fixed regard behold all things before
them grow transparent.

And that is why I was silent and my language is like
the shadowy sigh caught in the fold of shells.

IVORS: O my father, where have you hidden all this
time?

COEVRE: I disappeared. And in the depths of study I
found another birth.

I reappear in this hour of hesitation, and, on the ruin
of the city of dreams, I come to firmly establish
certitude.

IVORS: What is this costume in which I see you?

COEUVRE: I am bishop. I am priest among all men.

IVORS: Bishop!

What? Does that old superstition still exist?

GÉRIN: It exists, but secretly.

THYRSÉE: Oats sprouts where holy water once was kept.
The tabernacles are overgrown with weeds.

One does not know what has become of it. Not even
if there is still a pope. They have an old man no
longer since the last

Closed his old eyes in which were mirrored a multitude
of candles,

Like a fresh page under the lamp.

IVORS: I am seized with astonishment.

O Coeuvre! You! Who would have ever dreamed to
see you marshal this flock?

COEUVRE: Would I have believed it myself?

But he who bears his soul within him,

Not like a full-fed cow that ruminates on its feet,

But like a virgin mare, her mouth on fire with salt that
she has taken in the hand of her master,

How would he know the way to manage and constrain
her, the great and terrible thing that rears and
squeals in the narrow stable of his personal will,

When through the chinks of the door with the wind of
dawn there comes the smell of grass?

By what devious ways has it not conducted me? What
tasks were not imposed upon us?

And at last, behold, I have come to where I am.

Hearken to me, O my son, and you who are with him,
give ear!

IVORS: You too, are you going to promise us happiness?
We are weary of promises. I want the solidity of
the present certitude,

Though it only be the horizon I embrace, the hand
of my companion that I seize, the earth I have beneath my feet. These ruins are, at least, stones.

(*To* GÉRIN.

Draw the sword of Avare! Hold the blade erect before me that it may give me aid

Like an incorruptible witness in this place of prostitu-
tion.

COEUVRE: O my son, the sword has performed its task.
The moment for strife and litigation is past (I hear
the song of the lark!)

If the sun arises, all in vain will you cross your steel
with his impassive rays.

Hear my single voice reverberate in the immensity!

The winds are hushed, and alone with me in the supreme heights is heard this feeble song.

Look at the cleansed and wholesome earth about you,
consider the unlimited expanse, the day with the
purity of the night, the splendour of the Lion in
the limpidity of winter, and know that all things are
unveiled!

Do you not see that all is prepared for peace, and you
could no longer withhold the truce and pact?

The light commences, the air *takes* from one end to the
other! Behold the lateral presence of the sun, the
invasion irresistible of fire!

Behold the expanse, behold the glory, behold the day

of the showing-forth of God, like the victory of the
summer!

IVORS: I await you at that word and at that name.

Who is this of whom you speak? God? I do not
hear him, I do not see him, fixing upon him my eyes.
He eludes the investigation of my spirit.

What have I to do with him since I do not know him,
and tell me how

I shall learn this thing that I cannot understand.

COEUVRE: I do not know, my son, and precisely this is
my grief.

And this that, beside the amethyst, laughs on my finger like a star, that blue stone given by Besme the
day of his death.

Have we not a right

Not to see God? And I cannot shut it out.

He does not proffer words, and whence comes this
thing I hear?

I cannot attain it and yet it is with me.

It is nowhere and I should not know in what manner
to escape it, taking my way to the right or to the left.
In this, that I do not know it, I recognize it.

It is useless, then, to argue with the Master, for I tell
you he is pitiless, and unjust, and wholly deaf to
reason;

But we must attune ourselves to him and know, O my
son, what he wishes.

IVORS: How shall we know it, pray, if he has no word
to proclaim it?

100

COEUVRE: Well put, well put. But the whirlpool
   wherein an imprudent swimmer is caught,
Or the tiger that holds a hog beneath its paw, needs
   no word or phrase to make itself understood.
How shall we know what he wishes? But perhaps
   what he wishes is ourselves.
IVORS: What does he wish of us?
COEUVRE: I fear, O my son, there is no part of us escapes his covetousness. Have I not said that he is
   pitiless?
Each thing that lives, being born,
Is capable of combustion and burns at the approach
   of fire (the image decomposing according to its
   type);
And you see that the flame does not choose its nourishment, but finds all things acceptable, wood and or-
   dure, flowers and fruits, hair and fat.
But immortal man is susceptible to a flame unquencha-
   ble, wherein his being entire
Is consumed, consuming itself.
I will deplore this avarice of the Creator who desires
   to lose no atom of his creature and to recover the
   principal with interest. I accuse the treachery
Of this inner assent that he has planted in us like an
   ignited seed.
IVORS: That which we know as love?
COEUVRE: Yes, and there the iniquity is chiefly manifest.
For how far does he fall short of woman in being the
   adequate object of our love?

To whom, in the sacred embrace, shall we restore, as to
    the wedded spouse,
The life that we owe to the mother?
Why has he not permitted us to find satisfaction in the
    woman?
Whence comes this disagreement between the senses,
    this irreducible separation?
And what right can he evince
That we should love him when we do not know him?

IVORS: Will you deny that he escapes our senses?

COEUVRE: What a word you employ, *escapes!* As-
    suredly,
For three of our senses at least what you wish to say
    is true.
Nevertheless perhaps
He is not unknown to our taste (as the poet in his
    mouth, without speaking, distinguishes words by
    their savour),
And the heart is aware of its contact.

IVORS: You will strive in vain to disquiet me.
He who for ten long years has seen his death only a
    breath away, he who survives a shattered world,
Possesses his soul in prudence and will not easily yield
    it to each phrase making perfidious solicitation.
My charge is to administer the present, and what per-
    tains to the future cannot touch me.
I think that there does not exist for man any absolute
    happiness, that all seduction is vain,
And that in this scattered people you behold there is no
    point of perfect order!

Then in peace let each man eat his rightful bread.

COEUVRE: In this prudence I detect a truly royal heart.

You are right, O Ivors, not to turn your face towards
the future or the past,

But to envisage the present with straight regard, for
only the present exists, being the outer semblance
of the permanent eternity.

Yet I say to you, young eagle, that your eye, still weak,
is stopped at the envelope,

But the old griffin's glance knows how to search the
entrails of the earth and to discover mines and
treasures there.

Happiness is not some luxurious ornament;

It is in us like ourselves, it is blent with the subject of
our consciousness,

Infused with the incommunicable joy, with our interior
sensibility, with the very mode of our welfare!

Whence does it come that in nothing does it recognise
its object and that in all pleasure we feel

A perversion of the instinct, an idle recreation?

But happiness, where is it?   It is a smile that effaces itself, a voice that in ceasing makes itself heard, a
rape,

A precarious transport, and the ravishment of our discovery is mingled with our sobs.

Inquietude nothing lulls to rest!   Whence springs

This evil?   What is this fatal sentence?

O Ivors, if you take away our joy, will you deprive us
also of our pain?

At least our distress belongs to us alone, we shall not be despoiled of this heritage.

From the invalid condemned, the lover betrayed by his mistress, the widow who longs for her son, to die between his arms, the poet crushed by the feet of the multitude,

Do not withdraw the right to mourn their sorrow.

Do not take away our grief!

For it is our legitimate possession and every man on earth

Partakes of it, rich or poor, being subject to the heritage of death,

Our possession, and our defence, and our nourishment, and our stay, and our eye in the inextricable shades.

IVORS: O priest, on whom shall we lay the blame?

COEUVRE: All rupture of equilibrium presupposes a cause, and if no other resting-place is found admits of re-establishment.

Yet, as saith the Book, we know

That all in the first man have fallen away from primal blessedness,

But our hope is based in our punishment, happiness in our anguish, knowledge in our shades, salvation in our respite.

Man having been lured from his first allegiance to God, must be again restored.

IVORS: What do you mean?

COEUVRE: I mean *substituted*.

No man could have offered anything to God except the man that he is, in all his imperfection,

And not that through which he is man, through which
    he lives, that is to say the image of God.
God alone can give back God to God,
And that is why you read that he has made himself
    man.

IVORS: Priest, do not talk to us of these vague and an-
    cient things; it wearies us with keeping our heads
    turned backwards.
All the past was a part of that house which we have
    overthrown.
Free and bare, we should confront with open gaze
The new sky, the abyss of azure, the prodigy of that
    thing which is the dawn!
If some message is intended for our ears let it be made
    to us who are alive!
We do not ask that the sepulchre bear witness.

COEUVRE: Ivors, what is this defiance of the past?
    For me the present is so enormous that nothing can
    cease to be a part of it,
What we name history
Is not a succession of useless images, but the develop-
    ment, in so far as things going forth from time cease
    to belong thereto,
Of an order and a composition.
When a man reads there's progress in his reading,
But in the knowledge that he thence derives there is no
    other sequence than that from principle to conse-
    quences.
But why do I waste my soul in idle words?
The open wound in the flesh, what more immediate?

O my son, you would not know the way to extract the
ancient dart, you would not know how to heal the
ancient wound!

O Ivors, 'tis in vain you would be King and would dis-
pose all things with novelty, and that the society of
all men would breathe

The order proceeding from your mouth.

You would not know how to efface from your heart
a certain image.

And that image is no other than the one imprinted on
the linen of the veronica.

'Tis a visage fine and long, and the beard surrounds
the chin with a triple tuft.

Its expression is so austere that it frightens, and so holy

That the old sin within us organized

Trembles to its original root, and so profound is the
grief it shows

That, stunned, we are like the children who watch their
father weep, without understanding, *he* weeps!

In vain you would wish, O Ivors, to unroll before those
eyes the glory and the splendour of this world.
Those eyes, which, uplifted, with their gaze fash-
ioned the Universe,

Are downcast now, and rigorous tears descend;

From the brow sweat drops of blood.

But O my son, consider the mouth of thy God, the
mouth, O my son, of the Word,

What bitterness it savours now, what word ineffable
to even itself it tastes,

For the lips at the right hand corner gape in a tortured
smile.

How he weeps with all his being, letting the saliva escape like a child!

There is no bread for us, my son, while still we leave
this grief uncomforted.

It is the grief of the Son of Man who wishes to taste
and invest our crime,

It is the grief of the Son of God

That he could not offer his Father all mankind in the
mystery of the ostension.

> (IVORS *remains silent for a moment with bowed
> head, then he turns towards* GÉRIN *and*
> THYRSÉE, *and at last, straightening up and
> looking* COEUVRE *in the face, he says,*

So be it!

COEUVRE: Man, do you believe? Will you believe in
the Church which is the Word made visible?

IVORS: That is my wish.

COEUVRE: God!

IVORS: I believe in him.

COEUVRE: I believe in one sole living God, I believe in
one sole eternal God,

Distinct, creator, simple, in the plenitude of a triple
person,

And in Jesus-Christ, his only son, our Lord, true God
and true man,

One sole Christ in the hypostatical union, as in the
mystery of the generation;

Who was born of the Virgin Mary, suffered under
    Pontius Pilate, died, and the third day rose again;
And in the vivifying Holy Spirit, and in the Holy Cath-
    olic Church, infallible and exclusive;
And in the resurrection of the flesh, and in everlasting
    life; and in one sole baptism.

IVORS: I believe all this.

COEUVRE (*to all the others*): And you, what do you be-
    lieve?

THYRSÉE (*to* IVORS): O leader, we believe in your com-
    mand.

COEUVRE: O God, accept these bloodstained hands!
    accept these priests of sacrifice!
For they have performed a task acceptable in thy sight,
    abasing the beast that was seated between the hills,
    the city of Henoch, the monster of the horrible and
    laborious dream,
The grovelling hydra, the City, vomiter of smoke!
    And now in the place of the formless cry,
Lo, the revelation of the proffered word; and in the
    place of dreams
The truth and the reality of that which is.

IVORS: I believe.
And for baptism I salute that light effulgent and vir-
    ginal,
In which at this moment our globe is swallowed up.
I believe in God, and, with one hand laying hold of the
    hilt of my sword,
I stretch towards the lands whose backs are towards
    the sun

108

The other hand in the gesture of an oath!
Teach me, O my father, how I shall found among men
a new society.
According to the rigour of joy establishing a city in the
full glory of the evidence.

COEUVRE: Do not think that I offer a sovereign recipe
and that for all mankind accord and justice reside
In the virtue of an automatic arrangement.
But the incomprehensible Verity
Is like the sun in vision from whose radiance all things,
In the drunkenness of joy and the exultation of show-
ing forth his praise,
Derive their form and their life.

THYRSÉE: O sage, do not speak to Ivors of the light for
he loves it only too ardently even now and it alone
has power to make him laugh!
Lest he think of us no more, all glowing and flushed
with light like a crystal goblet filled with transparent
water!
Bid him rather turn his face towards us who love him
and towards the poor and the unfortunate.
But this young heart is not sustained by human sym-
pathies.

IVORS: Who will be so hard as to reproach me for lov-
ing the beautiful light?
But do not say I am not capable of also loving you.
You, my friends, and you, O my unhappy people!
And should you wish me to do nothing else than work
for my people's happiness
Tell me how I ought to act and where commence.

But what you name the happiness of man, welfare or
    what you will,

I have said that it was not an end in itself but rather
    the effect, by relation to that end, of an exact disposi-
    tion.

O my father, finish what I wish to say, for here my
    knowledge halts.

COEUVRE: The assembly of all mankind may be com-
    pared to a single man alone.

And as the Christian consecrates to his Maker that por-
    tion of the world in which he lives, it is thus that the
    Universe entire was placed between the hands

Of Man that thereby he might the more do homage.

For such is the reason of his nature, such is this whim
    of God's, after the bland negation of the Angels,

That the spirit should wed with Nothingness and force
    the inertness of matter to confession.

And if you ask me to portray the form

Of that new city on Earth beneath the sun of God,

I will simply say: today is as yesterday, all things are
    spread before us,

And in this temple which is the world no one will ever
    know how to escape the necessity of the ample cere-
    mony.

Let them simply open their eyes to what they do and let
    them acquiesce

To this mystery in which they participate.

And, in truth, if society is a body, in order that it now
    may live,

It must first be complete with all its organs.

And this is the function of those men and women
    scorned by the brutal part,
Open above the spirit, like the cavity of the profound
    chest, the choir of the corporal church,
Like nostrils that expand above the smoke of incense.
And other men are like the diligent feet and the hands,
    and like the eyes that scrutinise and seek, and like
    the brain, and the universe entire is the stuff of their
    industry,
And as the individual body grinds food between the
    jaws and receives it in the magazines and the store-
    rooms profound of the stomach, of the liver, and of
    the intestines,
It is so the social body absorbs, eliminates, digests.
And what is the king, the sacred being, the one among
    all men, the king,
If not the heart that is placed in the midst of the or-
    gans?
Like an altar whereon all matter comes to consume it-
    self, each stroke that it beats,
Presents all the blood in burning marriage to the celes-
    tial air,
Sending life to the far extremities of the organs.
O my soul, when I was a poet among the people
I invented those verses possessing no meter nor rhyme,
And I defined, in the secret of my heart, this function,
    double and reciprocal,
Through which man absorbs life and restores, in the
    act supreme of expiration,
An intelligible word.

And likewise social life is only the double verse of the *action* of grace or hymn,

By which humanity absorbs the leader and restores again his image.

> (*For some moments* LALA *has been visible at the corner of a ruin.*
>
> GÉRIN *points in her direction.*

IVORS (*letting his eyes fall upon her*): Who is this?

GÉRIN: That woman, Lala, your mother.

IVORS: Is it you, woman?

LALA: Who? Tell me, Ivors, that I may know it.

IVORS: The Queen of Madness, the mother of this erring multitude,

The Nymph of the human forest, she that promises peace in nourishment.

Today you see your work, these peoples overthrown, this city laid in the dust,

This form of humanity broken and disjointed, and these last remains that seek each other through the fallow fields.

O witch, man was not made to turn his face towards the reflecting sea.

Waters rise from the illimitable abyss, vertigo by night and by day, consternation and dream,

But it is enough for him to have earth beneath his feet, that he may cultivate it,

And the heaven above his head, computed by an exact astronomy.

LALA: O Ivors, these fools did not understand my words.

None knows the secret of my joy, neither they nor the others nor yourselves.

Coeuvre himself, though the only man who has possessed me,

(And you are the fruit of our union, O King!)

Has not known me all entire.

For his spirit attaches itself to causes, and, in the profound cavity of his spirit, he marshals them like clouds whence escape the lightning and the thunder.

But delight and this delicious rapture

Of feeling that one is freed from everything, this, as yet, he does not know.

The fixed flight of thought which, like a swimmer borne by a rapid current,

Maintains itself in the vibration of light

These sudden flights, these immeasurable leaps, these departures,

You are, as yet, ill versed in these, O pontiff!

For Coeuvre is not like a bird, but like a lion who goes towards the ford, and like a mighty horse hitched to the car of Jupiter,

But I am like a bird that one hears but does not see.

Each man is glad to attach his meaning to my song.

IVORS: Woman, your place is not with us.

LALA: It is true that my hair is grey and that soon the night and the gold will be banished by the mysterious colour of the snow.

But my beauty remains the same.

And Age that lays its hand upon me has dissipated the

old misunderstanding between those who pursue me
and myself.

Do you believe I have no place among you?

I am the promise that cannot be carried out and in that
very fact resides my charm.

I am the sweetness of that which is with the regret of
that which is not.

I am truth with the face of error and he who loves me
is not concerned with dividing the one from the
other.

He who hears me is cured of repose forever and of the
thought that he has found it.

He who looks in my eyes will desire no other face, and
what will he do if I smile?

He who has set himself to follow me will not know
how to stop.

But I feel that death is near!

Let the autumn come, let the instant approach of the
profound silence

When in the top of the tree the withered leaf

Seems to resound if it trembles,

And as a dead man rises towards the surface of the
pool, with the vibration of a cannon-shot,

It is thus, having made myself ready that this slight
noise

Will suffice to disengage my soul.

Farewell, Coeuvre, my husband.   Farewell, Ivors, my
son.

(She goes out.

114

IVORS: As for us establishing ourselves in the centre of
the City we will constitute the laws.

(They go out.   Noon.